# FOREWORD

Through their RD&D budgets, IEA Governments have supported the development of new energy technologies. These efforts have provided more energy-efficient, cleaner technologies. Many of these technologies, however, are still too expensive for commercial deployment. For them, the policy focus is therefore shifting from publicly supported research and development to measures to bring the technologies to the market.

The changing focus raises questions regarding government deployment programmes and the role of such programmes in $CO_2$-mitigation policies. Analytical tools are required to resolve these questions; experience curves are one such tool.

Experience curves demonstrate that investment in the deployment of emerging technologies could drive prices down so as to provide new competitive energy system for $CO_2$ stabilisation. This process of technology learning requires long-term, stable policies for energy technology. Considerable investments – known as "learning investments" – may be required over the next few decades. These may call for concerted action among governments.

The findings presented in this book have led to new IEA initiatives. Experience-curve analysis for policy-making was the subject of an IEA Workshop in Stuttgart in May 1999. Appendix 2 reproduces the workshop's recommendations, including a call on the IEA to initiate international collaboration on experience curves for energy technology policy. With the support of the IEA Committee on Energy Research and Technology (CERT), the Secretariat convened the first meeting under this rubric in Paris in October 1999. Appendix 3 presents results.[1]

This book was written by Professor Clas-Otto Wene, who is on leave of absence from the chair of Energy Systems Technology, at Chalmers University of Technology, Göteborg, Sweden.

The IEA Secretariat thanks the Swedish Government for its voluntary contributions to provide resources for this work.

*Robert Priddle*
*Executive Director*

---

1. See also: www.iea.org/excetp/excetp1.htm

# TABLE OF CONTENTS

## List of Figures and Tables

### Figures

## *Tables*

# CHAPTER 1: RIDING ON THE EXPERIENCE CURVE

> *The experience curve is a long-range strategic rather than a short-term tactical concept. It represents the combined effects of a large number of factors ... ... it cannot be used reliably for operating controls or short-term decision making. But in the formulation of competitive strategy, the experience curve is a powerful instrument, indeed.*
>
> D.L.Bodde, "Riding the Experience Curve", Technology Review, March/April 1976.

## Price for an Emerging Technology

### Experience improves performance

Operating in competitive markets makes individuals, enterprises and industries do better. This fact is at the heart of the experience-curve phenomenon. Price is the most important measure of performance for new energy technologies. In this book, we will therefore focus on how learning through market experience reduces prices for various energy technologies and how these reductions influence the dynamic competition among technologies. We will also demonstrate how the energy policy-maker can exploit the experience-curve phenomenon to set targets and to design measures to make new technologies commercial. The Kyoto Protocol on greenhouse gas reductions has given a new sense of urgency to energy technology policy and the examples selected are relevant to this quest. A major theme in this book is that experience curves provide powerful tools for formulating low-cost strategies to reduce and stabilise $CO_2$ emissions during the next decades.

In order to make available environmentally effective technologies which are price competitive, governments support these technologies, both through funding of research and development (R&D) and through price subsidies or other forms of deployment policy. The focus in this book is on deployment support. Such support is considered legitimate because prices are expected to fall as producers and users gain experience. Crucial questions concern how much support a technology needs to become competitive and how much of this support has to come from government budgets. Experience curves make it possible to answer such questions because they provide a simple, quantitative

## *The experience curve equation*

The trend line in Figure 1.1 is a fit of a power function to the measured points. It is this line which is commonly referred to as the "experience curve". The curve is described by the following mathematical expression.

$$\text{Price at year t} = P_0 * X^{-E}$$

"$P_0$" is a constant equal to the price at one unit of cumulative production or sales. In Figure 1.1, $P_0$ is the price at 1 MW of cumulative sales and is equal to 32 US\$(1992)/$W_p$. "X" is cumulative production or sales in year t. X in Figure 1.1 is the sum total in MW of all PV-Modules sold worldwide until the year t. For instance, in the year t = 1992 the price is 5.9 US\$/$W_p$ and the sum of all sales until 1992 is 340 MW. "E" is the (positive) experience parameter, which characterises the inclination of the curve. Large values of E indicate a steep curve with a high learning rate. The relation between the progress ratio, PR, discussed in the text and the experience parameter is

$$PR = [P_0 * (2X)^{-E}] / [P_0 * X^{-E}] = 2^{-E}$$

The experience parameter for the curve in Figure 1.1 is E = 0.29, which gives a progress ratio of $2^{-0.29} = 0.82$ or 82%.

relationship between price and the cumulative production or use of a technology. There is overwhelming empirical support for such a price-experience relationship from all fields of industrial activities, including the production of equipment that transforms or uses energy.[2]

Figure 1.1 shows the experience curve for photovoltaic modules on the world market for the period 1976-1992. The data indicate a steady, progressive decrease in prices through cumulative sales, which are used as the measure of the experience accumulated within the industry. The relationship remains the same over three orders of magnitude. The data are presented in the usual way for experience curves, namely in a double-logarithmic diagram. This is the representation used throughout this book. With this representation it is possible to follow the experience

**Figure 1.1. Experience Curve for PV Modules, 1976-1992**

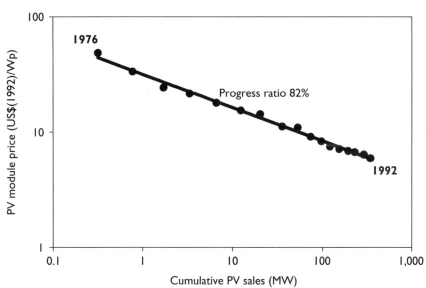

Experience curve for photovoltaic modules on the world market. The price for a module is given in constant 1992 US$ per peak watt, $W_p$. Peak watts are the power output from the module at optimum solar conditions as defined by certification agencies. Adopted from Williams and Terzian (1993).

---

2. See Boston Consulting Group (1968) or Abell and Hammond (1979).

effect over many orders of magnitude. However, the decisive advantage of this method is that the experience curve becomes a simple straight line in a double-logarithmic diagram, making it easy to identify the experience effect and, as we shall see, spot structural changes in markets or technologies. Appendix A further explains the properties of a double-logarithmic representation.

The straight line captures a very important feature of the experience curve. Anywhere along the line, an increase by a fixed percentage of the cumulative production gives a consistent percentage reduction in price. In the literature, comparisons between different experience curves are made by doubling the cumulative volume; the corresponding change in price is referred to as the *progress ratio*. The experience curve in Figure 1.1 has a progress ratio of 82%, meaning that price is reduced to 0.82 of its previous level after a doubling of cumulative sales. The extensive literature on experience curves generally uses the term progress ratio, but in this book we will also use the term *learning rate*, which is (100 − Progress Ratio). The learning rate for PV modules in the period 1976-1992 was thus 18% (=100-82), meaning that each doubling of sales reduced the price by 18%.

The progress ratio and learning rate are the same for any part of the simple experience curve in Figure 1.1. This means that young technologies learn faster from market experience than old technologies with the same progress ratios. The same absolute increase in cumulative production will have more dramatic effect at the beginning of a technology's deployment than it will later on. Market expansion from 1 to 2 MW reduces prices by 18% in the example in Figure 1.1, but at a volume of 100 MW, the market has to deploy another 100 MW to obtain another 18% price reduction.

For well-established technology, such as coal power plants using conventional technology, the volume required to double cumulative sales may be of the order of 1000 GW, so the experience effect will hardly be noticeable in stable markets. We will discuss how structural changes in the market or technological innovations may change this picture. However, even fundamental changes in established technology, such as fluidised bed or advanced thermodynamic cycles, will only affect distinct components or functions of the technology, leaving others basically intact. The new components will learn rapidly from market experience, but they only represent a part of the total cost for the technology. The observed experience effect of such grafted technology is therefore less than for emerging new technologies, such as photovoltaics.

Wind power is an example of a technology which relies on technical components that have reached maturity in other technological fields. The experience curve for wind turbines in Figure 1.2 shows a modest progress ratio of 96%, corresponding to a learning rate of 4%. Neij (1999) suggests that most of the progress is due to progressive increase in turbine size. Other sections of this book will show that experience curves for the total process of producing electricity from wind are considerably steeper than for wind turbines. Such experience curves reflect the learning in choosing sites for wind power, tailoring the turbines to the site, maintenance, power management, etc, which all are new activities.

**Figure 1.2.  Danish Wind Turbines, 1982-1997**

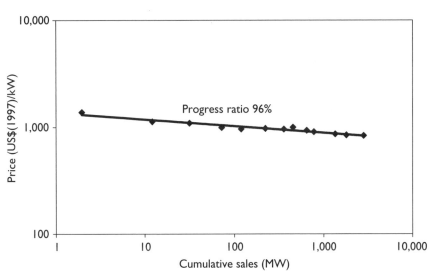

Experience curve for wind turbine produced by Danish manufacturers.  Adopted from Neij (1999).

The literature on experience curves provides benchmarks for the progress ratio from other fields of technology. Figure 1.3 shows the distribution of progress ratios from 108 observed cases in manufacturing firms. The average value and the most probable value for the distribution are both 82%. Industry-level progress ratios have a similar distribution. The average progress ratio at the level of the individual firm is equal to the ratio measured for modules in the photovoltaic industry as a whole in the period 1976-1992. Wind turbines, with a progress ratio of 96%, lie on the upper tail of the distribution. Low progress ratios, or high learning rates, are observed for semiconductor technology, e.g., production of integrated circuits shows a progress ratio of 72% (Ayres and Martinas, 1992). Miniaturisation may partially explain the low progress ratios for the semiconductor industry.

**Figure 1.3. Distribution of Progress Ratios**

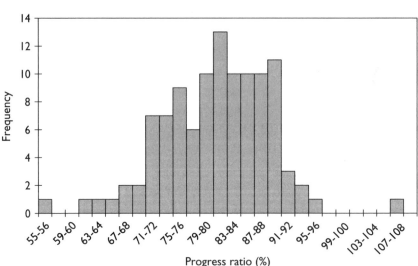

Progress ratios for 108 cases observed in 22 field studies. The studies estimated the behaviour of cost with cumulative volume in firms and include manufacturing processes in industries such as electronics, machine tools, system components for electronic data processing, papermaking, aircraft, steel, apparel, and automobiles. Industry-level progress ratios are excluded. The outlayers at 55-56% and 107-108% indicate cases where cost decreased by 44-45% and increased by 7-8%, respectively, for each doubling of cumulative volume. Adopted from Dutton and Thomas (1984).

## Assessing Future Prospects

Existing data show that experience curves provide a rational and systematic methodology to describe the historical development and performance of technologies. We use them to assess the prospects for future improvements in the performance of a technology. The curves show that cumulative production for the market reduces prices. Assessments of future prospects are therefore particularly important in developing deployment policies for environmentally friendly technologies. We will use the example of photovoltaics to demonstrate the use of the experience curve methodology for policy analysis.

Figure 1.4 indicates how learning acquired through cumulative production reduces the cost of photovoltaic modules. For photovoltaic systems to compete against central power stations, the cost of modules

**Figure 1.4. Making Photovoltaics Break-Even**

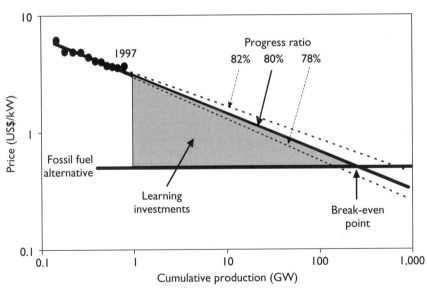

Break-even point and learning investments for photovoltaic modules with a progress ratio of 80%. The shaded area indicates the remaining learning investments to reach the break-even point. The figure also shows changes in the break-even point for progress ratios of 78% and 82%.

has to be brought down to 0.5 US$/W$_p$, indicated by the "Fossil fuel alternative" line in the diagram. Updating and expanding the experience-curve analysis in Figure 1.1 until 1997 lowers the progress ratio for the modules to 80%. Extrapolating the experience curve over future cumulative production levels of modules shows that to break even with fossil fuel technology requires cumulative production of about 200 GW. However, there are niche markets that may act as stepping stones for the descent to break even with currently cost-efficient technologies. The use of such niche markets in designing technology policy will be discussed in Chapter 3.

The experience curve shows the investment necessary to make a technology, such as PV, competitive, but it does not forecast *when* the technology will break-even. The time of break-even depends on deployment rates, which the decision-maker can influence through policy. With historical annual growth rates of 15%, photovoltaic modules will reach break-even point around the year 2025. Doubling the rate of growth will move the break-even point 10 years ahead to 2015.

Investments will be needed for the ride down the experience curve, that is for the learning efforts which will bring prices to the break-even point. An indicator for the resources required for learning is the difference between actual price and break-even price, i.e., the *additional* costs for the technology compared with the cost of the same service from technologies which the market presently considers cost-efficient. We will refer to these additional costs as *learning investments*[3], which

---

3. In the case of an emerging new electric technology without fuel cost, such as PV, the specific learning investment, LI, per kW of capacity is

$$LI = P(new) - [8760*\rho*p(market) - O\&M]/annuity$$

P(new) is the price per kW for the emerging new technology at the time of investment and p(market) is the price per kWh of electricity from the currently cost-efficient (fossil fuel) technology. $\rho$ is the load factor and O&M are the operation and maintenance costs at the break-even point for power plants with the new technology. The second term is the break-even price. More detailed calculations of learning investments therefore require databases with time series not only of technology prices and installations, but also of market prices and interest rates. Throughout this book we will assume that the break-even price stays constant during the whole learning period. This assumption usually provides a good first approximation to estimate the magnitude of learning investments for the technologies discussed here. Compare, for instance, our assumption of a constant break-even price with the curve for supercritical coal in Figure 1.5.

means that they are investments in learning to make the technology cost-efficient, after which they will be recovered as the technology continues to improve.

The remaining learning investments for photovoltaic modules are indicated by the shaded triangle in Figure 1.4. The sum of all future learning investments needed to bring module technology to the break-even point indicated in the figure is 60 billion US$. This is a substantial investment in learning, considering the learning investments of 3-4 billion US$ made in PV modules until 1998. The challenge is to put policies in place which mobilise resources on the market for these investments. Public demonstration programmes and subsidies can only seed this process. The learning investments do include the cost of research and development activities carried out by the commercial market actors, who ultimately have to recover those costs through market revenues. Means of obtaining learning investments, for instance through electricity feed laws or by stimulating niche markets, will be discussed in Chapter 3.

Learning investments are primarily provided through market mechanisms, and they always involve commercial actors on the market. There may be some overlap between learning investments and government expenditures for research, development and demonstration (RD&D), because experimental or demonstration plants may be financed from the public RD&D budget (IEA/OECD, 1997). In specific cases, involving smaller programmes, government expenditures may be a substantial part of total learning investments. However, for major technologies such as photovoltaics, wind power, biomass, or heat pumps, resources provided through the market dominate the learning investments. Government *deployment* programmes may still be needed to stimulate these investments. The government expenditures for these programmes will be included in the learning investments.

Although there may be occasional overlaps, we find that the terms "learning investments" and "public RD&D" refer to different parts of the resources needed for technology learning. It is therefore not surprising that until today the RD&D spending on photovoltaics by the IEA countries was twice as large as the learning investments. Public RD&D

spending can initiate and support the initial stages in developing a major new technology. If the technology appears valuable and marketable, deployment may start and learning investments will then provide an increasing share of the resources for technology improvements. We thus expect learning investments to become the dominant resource for later stages in technology development, where the objectives are to overcome cost barriers and make the technology commercial.

Figure 1.4 indicates some of the uncertainties in our estimates of break-even points and learning investments. A progress ratio of 80% represents a best fit to available information. But this information is also consistent with progress ratios of 78% and 82%, which would indicate break-even at 150 GW and 600 GW and learning investments of 40 billion US$ and 120 billion US$.

The uncertainties in the estimates of break-even point and learning investments are enhanced by the extrapolation of the experience curve over more than two orders of magnitude. These uncertainties will be resolved as experience about photovoltaics accumulates. Beside numerical precision, an extrapolation must consider also other sources of uncertainty, which will be considered in the next chapter. For instance, it is important to measure the experience curve under stable market conditions. Like all forecasting methodologies, experience curves have to be used with prudence. One of the basic messages of this book is that the experience curve methodology should be embedded in a continuous process of policy analysis and evaluation, where it will serve as *an interactive tool for developing effective strategies* to make environmentally friendly technologies available to the energy system.

## Competition for Learning Opportunities

The experience effect irreversibly binds tomorrow's options to to-day's actions. Successful market implementation sets up a positive price-growth cycle; market growth provides learning and reduces price, which makes the product more attractive, supporting further growth which further reduces price, etc. Conversely, a technology which cannot enter the market because it is too expensive will be denied the learning necessary to overcome the cost barrier and therefore the technology will be *locked out* from the market. Consequently, the experience effect leads to a competition between technologies to take advantage of opportunities for learning provided by the market. To exploit the opportunity, the emerging and still too expensive technology also has to compete for learning investments.

The experience-curve phenomenon presents the policy-maker with both risks and potential benefits. The risks involve the lock-out of potentially low-cost and environmentally friendly technologies. The benefits lie in the creation of new energy technology options by exploiting the learning effect, e.g., through niche markets. However, there is also the risk that expected benefits will not materialise. Learning opportunities in the market and learning investments are both scarce resources. Policy decisions to support market learning for a technology must therefore be based on assessment of the future markets for the technology and its value to the energy system.

Figure 1.5 illustrates the use of learning opportunities in the power sector in the European Union. Policy measures have provided access to learning opportunities and stimulated learning investments for wind power, photovoltaics and biomass technology. Electricity from wind produced at the sites with best performance can today compete with electricity produced in coal-fired power plants. Photovoltaics and biomass technology require considerable improvements in performance before electricity from these technologies can compete with electricity from fossil fuel technology.[4]

Natural gas combined cycle persistently shows cost advantage over other technologies, which explains its dominant role in present investment decisions regarding electricity technology. The figure therefore illustrates the possibility of *lock-in* of natural gas technology

---

4. Internalising eventual external costs may change the competition between the technologies but has little influence on progress ratios.

within the European power sector. The fact that the world-wide capacity of natural gas combined cycle has increased from a few GW in 1985 to 150 GW in 1997 emphasises the possibility of a more general lock-in of gas technology. A technology lock-in is not intrinsically problematic; it may even be necessary for efficient learning. However, if future energy systems have to reduce their use of the technology, e.g., due to excessive fuel cost or environmental constraints, the cost of escaping the lock-in condition may be considerable. There will be costs related to changes in the system, but there may also be substantial opportunity costs if the lock-in has resulted in the exclusion or lock-out of other technology, e.g., renewable technology, that is required to meet future needs efficiently. The consequences of lock-in of gas technology for managing $CO_2$ reductions are discussed in Chapter 4.[5]

The risk of lock-out and the possibility of lock-in do not in themselves legitimise policy interventions. An important function of the market is to select winning technologies. In a market where prices reflect all present and future externalities, we expect the integrated action of the commercial actors to produce an efficient balance between technology lock-out and utilisation of technology options. This means that, in the absence of externalities, we expect the market mechanisms to allocate learning opportunities efficiently. This also means that market mechanisms are expected to provide learning investments for promising new technology.

The risk of climate change, however, poses an externality which might be very substantial and costly to internalise through price alone. Intervening in the market to support a climate-friendly technology that may otherwise risk lock-out may be a legitimate way for the policy-maker to manage the externality; the experience effect thus expands his policy options. For example, carbon taxes in different sectors of the economy can activate the learning for climate-friendly technologies by

---

5. For general discussions on lock-in, lock-out and entrenchment see e.g., Arthur (1990) and Cowan (1999). In this book, the term "lock-in" is used in a general sense referring to a situation where many individual decisions re-enforce learning and use of a specific technology and lead to a stable and dominating position for this technology. We will not make the distinction between "lock-in by small events" (Arthur, 1990) and "entrenchment" (Cowan, 1999).

## Figure 1.5. Electric Technologies in EU, 1980-1995

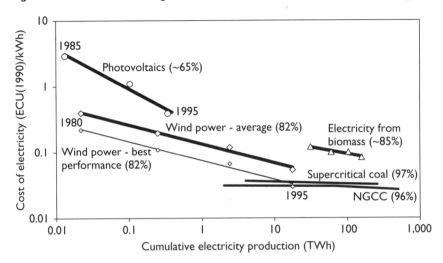

Cost of electricity and electricity produced from selected electric technologies installed in the European Union 1980-1995. Numbers in parentheses are estimates of progress ratios. Data for renewable technology are from the EU-ATLAS project. The curve for Natural Gas Combined Cycle (NGCC) is calculated for EU based on the information in Claeson (1999). The progress ratio for supercritical coal power plants is based on a US study of Joskow and Rose (1985). For the fossil technologies, the fuel prices have been set constant at the 1995 level. EU-ATLAS data are available for five-year intervals for the period 1980-1995 (Marsh, 1998) and do not permit more than very rough estimates of the progress ratios for photovoltaics and electricity from biomass.[6] The two curves for wind power show the average production cost and the production cost from the plants with the best performance.

raising the break-even price. The increased use of biomass for district heating in Sweden illustrated in Figure 1.6 is an example of the use of a carbon tax in the heating sector. For technologies which have costs far higher than their break-even costs, more targeted policies will be

---

6. The experience curve for electricity from photovoltaics seems much steeper than the curve for photovoltaic modules on the world market in Figures 1.1 and 1.4. There are several explanations for the apparent higher learning rate in the ATLAS data. One explanation is the change in PV applications in the period 1985-1995 from remote systems to grid-connected systems, which have substantially reduced cost for Balance of System (BOS), exaggerating the experience effect. Another explanation is that the EU was a late starter in 1980 compared with the US and Japan, and could rely on importing experience on PV during the 1980s. The latter explanation illustrates the distinction between global and regional experience curves. Both explanations indicate that the high rate of learning cannot be maintained, and that future progress ratios for electricity from PV in EU will depend on the global progress ratio for PV modules.

## Figure 1.6. District Heating in Sweden, 1980-1995

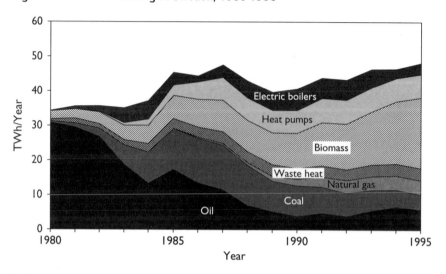

Fuels and technologies for production of district heating in Sweden. Since the introduction of carbon taxes for the heating sector, biofuels have increased their market shares by 70%, while coal has lost half its share. The fuel switch has considerably increased the learning opportunities for biomass technologies.

needed, such as subsidies and creation of niche markets. Chapter 4 will present modelling experiments, which suggest that using targeted energy technology policies to manage carbon emissions may be less expensive than requiring the whole economy to adjust to higher prices.

Environmentally friendly technologies compete among themselves for learning investments, both globally and locally. The policy-maker needs analysis to aid the selection of technologies for which learning opportunities should be created. Concentrating on only a few technologies may appear as an efficient strategy, but robust energy systems also require local flexibility and ability to manage the risk of technology failure. Chapter 4 discusses technology portfolios to handle the conflicting needs of coherent global learning and autonomous local deployment, and the use of experience curves to analyse such portfolios.

# The Purpose of this Book

The general purpose of this book is to demonstrate the potential of experience curves as tools to inform and strengthen energy technology policy. More specifically, we will apply experience curves to show how implementation of $CO_2$-benign technology presents feasible, low-cost paths to $CO_2$ stabilisation.

Experience curves remain under-developed tools for public energy policy, in spite of the rich literature on the phenomenon and the use of the curves as planning and management tools in technology-intensive industries. Experience curves can become powerful instruments for strategic analysis during most of the phases of policy-making. They support the identification of technology areas where intervention is necessary to avoid lock-in, the selection of realistic policy targets in these areas, and the design and monitoring of policy measures to reach the targets. Specifically, experience curves help the design and monitoring of portfolios of $CO_2$-benign technologies.

To widen the use of experience curves, quality assured data on the experience effect for energy technologies has to be made available, and case studies are required to demonstrate the use of experience curves for policy analysis. We will present case studies and also analyse experience curves. However, to establish experience curves as a public policy tool more work has to be done to collect data, to analyse experience curves for various technologies, and to provide case studies.

To avoid the pitfalls in constructing and interpreting an experience curve, some theoretical understanding of the phenomenon is necessary. A simple model of learning is therefore introduced in Chapter 2. This model is used to discuss the relation between public policies and technology learning, price and cost relationships manifested in experience curves and learning in compound systems. We will also discuss the effect on the experience curve of structural changes in the market or in the technology.

Chapter 3 presents three case studies on the use of experience curves to set policy targets and to design and monitor policy measures. We look at termination of RD&D support for demand-side technologies that have reached maturity, subsidies for wind power, and the creation of niche markets for photovoltaics. From the point of view of technology policy, technology development shows two distinct phases: a first phase dominated by public R&D support followed by a learning phase, where the technology acquires experience in the market to reach commercial maturity. The learning phase may require public deployment policies to provide the technology with learning opportunities in the market. An important question is how governments can stimulate learning investments from private sources.

In Chapter 4, we return to dynamic competition among technologies discussed in section 3 above. Modelling experiments with experience curves are used to develop pictures of future energy systems. These modelling experiments illustrate the risks of technology lock-out, but also the possibility to create low-cost energy systems that lead to stabilisation of $CO_2$ emissions by the middle of the next century. Models will help design technology portfolios and explore the effects of uncertainty about the shape of experience curves.

# CHAPTER 2:  LEARNING REQUIRES ACTION

*This chapter introduces a simple cybernetic model for learning and uses this model to relate technology learning to public policies for technology R&D and deployment. The model provides background for a discussion of price-cost relationships and causes for observed changes in progress ratios. It provides practical guidance on how to analyse compound learning systems, such as production of electricity from wind energy.*

## An Input-Output Model of Learning

The engineers and managers in the aeroplane industry were the first to define a quantitative expression for the observation that "Experience improves performance". In 1936, Wright published a seminal paper on "Factors affecting the cost of airplanes", where he discussed the functional relationship between cost and quantity (Wright, 1936). He found that cost reductions for different inputs to the production process could be described by the same mathematical expression. When plotted in log-log diagrams, costs for "Labor", "Material Purchased" and "Material Raw" as a function of cumulative production of aeroplanes appeared as straight lines with different inclinations, meaning that what we today call "progress ratios" were different. Wright's work was related to learning within a factory and his curves for inputs to the factory process became known as learning curves. Somewhat narrowly, the curves were described as reflecting "learning-by-doing", although "learning-by-producing" would have been more accurate.

Arrow (1962) drew the economic implications from "learning-by-doing". He generalised the experience effect and advanced as a hypothesis for economic studies, "that technical change in general can be ascribed to experience, that it is the very activity of production which gives rise to problems for which favorable responses are selected over time" (p. 156).

The experience-curve phenomenon was firmly established within the *management sciences* through the work of the Boston Consulting Group during the 1960s (Boston Consulting Group, 1968; Abell and Hammond, 1979). The original learning curves focused on the costs of individual inputs to the factory process. The Boston Consulting Group (BCG) looked at total cost and widened the inputs to the learning system to include "all of the cost elements which may have a trade-off against each other. This therefore means all costs of every kind required to deliver the product to the ultimate user, including the cost of intangibles which affect perceived value. There is no question that R&D, sales expenses, advertising, overhead, and everything else is included" (p. 12). BCG introduced the term experience curves for the curves relating *total* cost and cumulative quantity, and we will follow their terminology in this book. The term "learning curve" is used to indicate a relation between one of several, substitutable inputs and cumulative output.

With the introduction of experience curves, studies of the experience effect leave the factory to analyse instead market products and performance at industrial levels. The market approach means, however, that costs become increasingly difficult to measure. Most of the published experience curves therefore show how price is related to cumulative production. In a stable market with stable return on equity for the producer, the cost and price experience curves appear as two parallel lines in a log-log diagram. This means that the cost and price experience curves have the same progress ratio. The ratio between cost and price is fixed and reflects the return on equity within the industry.

The large literature on experience curves provides empirical information about the experience effect for a wide variety of industrial goods and services. This information offers benchmarks for experience curves for new technologies. In spite of the overwhelming empirical support for the experience curve, there is still no theoretical explanation for the form of the curve or the value of progress ratios. However, in order to be able to discuss what should constitute an experience curve, we need some simple model of the experience phenomenon. We use the fact that both learning and experience curves establish relations between the input and the output of a learning system.

Figure 1.1 shows the basic model for a learning system from cybernetic theory (Ashby, 1964). The learning system could be a factory production line for aeroplanes in the case of learning curves, or the industry for production and sales of PV modules in the case of experience curves. In a competitive market, the learning system considers the effects of output on its environment and adjusts its internal working to improve performance. The internal adjustment is based on earlier experience of transforming input to output, and the experience curve defines the measure of performance as the ratio of input over output. The total input is usually measured in monetary terms and the output in physical terms, so that the measure of performance is cost per unit, e.g. US$/kW, Euro/m$^2$ or Yen/kWh.

**Figure 2.1. Basic Model for a Learning System**

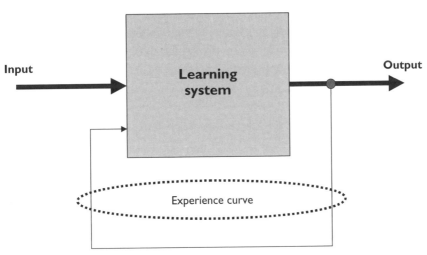

The experience curve is a measure of the efficiency of the feedback, or learning loop, for the system.

The model implies that learning is the result of activities producing outputs which are assessed by a competitive environment. Conversely, a system that has no output will not learn, meaning that a technology which is not produced and deployed cannot start the ride down the experience curve. Technologies cannot become cost-efficient by laboratory R&D alone.

The basic learning model does not make any hypothesis about the processes going on inside the learning system; in fact it considers this system as a black box for which only input and output can be observed.[7] The model is simple, but provides useful guidance for reflecting on the experience effect and for construction of experience curves.

In the next section, we will enter inside the black box in order to discuss the relationship between the experience effect and public policies for R&D and for deployment. Some experience curves show "knees" where the progress ratio changes. Causes for such changes may lie outside or inside the learning system, e.g., major changes in technology or in the market. Section 2.3 discusses how a major technological change may appear in the experience curve. Section 2.4 considers the market and how changes in the market may affect the relationship between price and cost. Section 2.5 elaborates on compound systems, i.e., when the learning system has two or more distinguishable systems, whose experience curves can be measured separately.

---

7. The input-output model for learning includes price reductions due to economies of scale. Critics of the experience curve concept have argued that the observed correlation could as well be explained by scale effects (see, e.g., Hall and Howell, 1985). Regarding the discussion on how to separate experience and scale effects, Abell and Hammond (1979, p. 114) note that "(t)he confusion arises because growth in experience usually coincides with growth in size of an operation". They conclude: "Usually the overlap between the two effects is so great that it is difficult (and not too important) to separate them. This is the practice we will adopt from here on (while remaining alert for those exceptions where scale effects can be achieved alone, such as in high fixed-cost, capital-intensive industries.)" We will follow the lead of Abell and Hammond in this book and not separate the two effects. This means that we accept that the experience curve may contain scale effects. In historical analysis such as in the two first case studies in the following chapter, the distinction between experience and scale effects is of no practical consequence. However, it is important to remain alert to scale effects when experience curves are used for technology forecasting and scenario analysis. The reason is that we expect scale effects to saturate while empirical data show experience effects remaining constant over many orders of magnitude.

# Influencing the Learning System: Public R&D and Deployment Policies

The relationship between public R&D spending and the experience curve phenomenon is an important concern for policy analysis. Watanabe (1995, 1999) provides insight into how public R&D seeds the industrial learning process, but also how public R&D efforts need to reach into and stimulate this process to achieve improvements in technology performance. This insight is also expressed in other research on innovation and technological change, notably in the innovation systems approach, where one of the cornerstones is that "interactions between firms, and between firms and other knowledge-producing agencies, are central to innovation performance" (Smith, 1996).

Figure 2.2. Influences on the Learning System from Public Policy

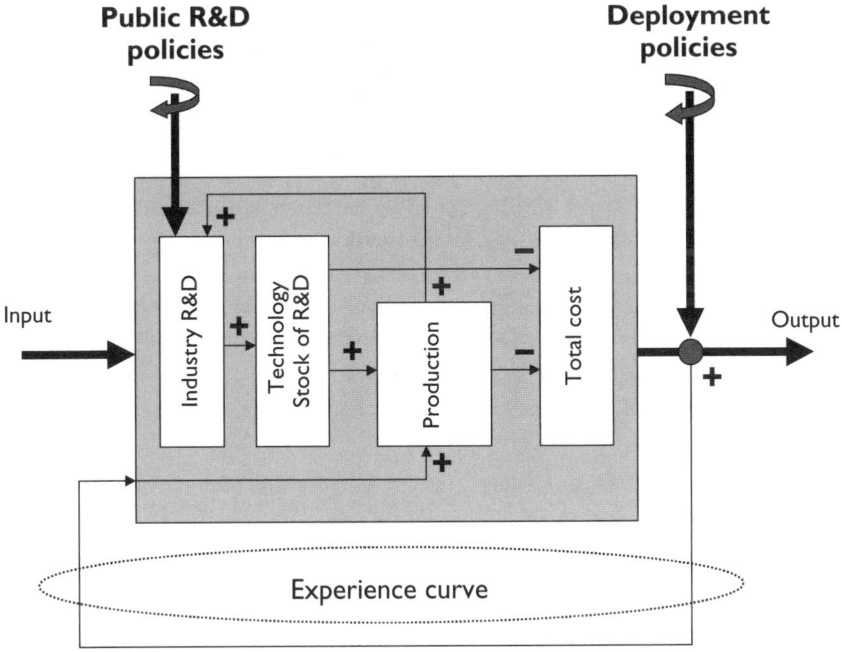

Factors influencing the total cost are taken from Watanabe (1999).

Figure 2.2 relies on the quantitative analysis by Watanabe (1999) of the factors contributing to the decrease in the cost of solar cell production in Japan in the period 1976-1990. Watanabe looks at the interactions between public and industry R&D, production and the technology stock created by PV technology R&D. The figure interprets his results in the basic learning model. The "+" and "–" identify a cycle, which includes the crucial elements of the experience curve. An increase in "Output" or sales increases "Production", which stimulates "Industry R&D", which enlarges "Technology Stock", which boosts "Production" and reduces "Total Cost", enhancing market opportunities and thus sales. The cycle reinforces itself; it is a "virtuous cycle". There is a double boost to production coming from the sales on the market and from the improvement in knowledge through R&D.

The technology stock of PV R&D accumulates the benefits of industrial R&D and reflects the cumulative character of technology learning. The easily observed cumulative output from the learning system acts as a proxy for this aspect of learning.[8] Watanabe's econometric analysis suggests that more than 70% of cost reductions were directly due to an increase in the stock of technology knowledge (Watanabe, 1995). The quantitative analysis of learning in producing PV-modules therefore supports the use in the experience curve of *cumulative* output as the variable against which performance should be measured.

Figure 2.2 shows that public R&D can seed the learning process within the industry but not directly influence total cost. In order to contribute to cost reductions and to the industrial stock of knowledge, the output from the public R&D process has to enter into the internal industry R&D process. The outstanding feature of this internal learning process is that there is no virtuous cycle and no substantial cost reductions without market interactions.

---

8. Watanabe's analysis also considers the fact that knowledge becomes obsolete or is "forgotten". A corresponding effect may be seen in experience curves. For instance, knowledge depreciation is suggested as the reason why Lockheed's cost for the L-1011 Tri-Star did not follow the usual learning pattern (Argote and Epple, 1990).

The analysis suggests a two-pronged technology policy. Firstly, technology policy requires public R&D to initiate research on uncertain technology options, which present a high investment risk, followed up by pre-competitive public R&D expenditures to seed the industry R&D process and keep it on track. Secondly, technology policy requires deployment measures to ensure market introduction of technologies which are not yet competitive.

Figure 2.3 is a roadmap for two-pronged energy technology policies. The roadmap describes how the risk of climate change can be managed by technology development. The road proceeds through three types of terrain, dominated by three categories of technologies. The arrow shows the direction to be taken for decarbonisation of the economy, and the fields in the arrow indicate the present status and the risks and opportunities for each category. The area below the arrow indicates mechanisms which are available to achieve technology development.

**Figure 2.3. A Roadmap for Policies on Decarbonisation Energy Technologies**

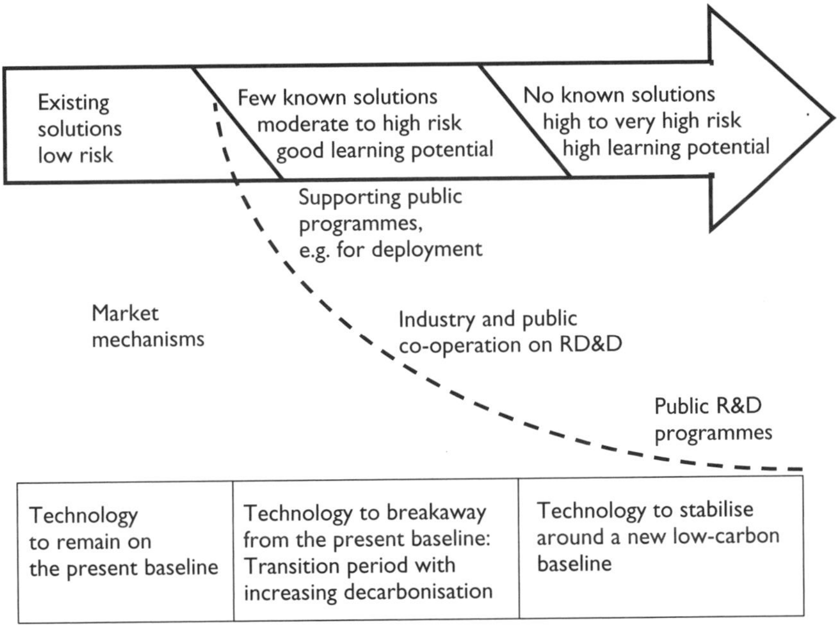

A dotted line divides the area into terrain where market mechanisms provide all the necessary learning opportunities and terrain where government R&D and deployment programmes may be needed.

The first category of technologies is "Technologies to remain on the present baseline". The baseline represents a business-as-usual case with no climate change policies in place. Historical data show that baseline technology led to considerable reductions in the carbon intensity of GDP. Nakicenovic (1996) determined that $CO_2$ emissions per unit of GDP in the US economy were reduced by 18% for each doubling of GDP during the period 1850-1990, which indicates a progress ratio of 82% for the decarbonisation of economic activities.[9] The baseline analysis presented in the World Energy Outlook (IEA, 1998) provides a progress ratio of 79% for decarbonisation of world GDP during the period 1971-2020. The roadmap states that there are existing technological solutions to remain on the present baseline. Examples of such low-risk solutions are advanced coal technologies, improved Otto-engines, combined cycle gas turbines and existing nuclear power technologies. For these technologies, development and deployment are internal industrial transactions steered by market mechanisms. The parent technologies have already come a long way down the experience curve, and the grafted technologies show low learning rates. However, the policy analyst has to monitor these experience curves because the technologies in this group provide benchmarks for the technologies in the two other groups.

To reach Kyoto targets and ultimately stabilise $CO_2$ emissions will require much higher rates of decarbonisation than what is observed for the baseline. Accelerated use of gas technologies can temporarily reduce the decarbonisation progress ratio below 80%, but will not by themselves lead to a breakaway from the current baseline. Long-term efforts to reduce the progress ratio require new climate-friendly

---

9. Nakicenovic (1996) reports a value of 76% based on cumulative input of carbon to the system. However, following our cybernetic model, learning is a function of cumulative output, i.e., cumulative GDP. Converting from cumulative carbon to cumulative GDP gives a progress ratio of 82%, which is equal to the most probable value found by Dutton and Thomas (1984), Figure 1.3.

technologies; e.g., wind power, electricity from biomass and compact fluorescent light (CFL). Photovoltaic and fuel cell technologies are on the early part of their experience curves and not yet fully commercial. They therefore need public support for their deployment and possibly co-operative R&D to improve their performance. For the policy analyst and decision-maker, experience curves provide tools to analyse the future markets for these technologies, to design efficient policy measures and to monitor the effects of these measures. The focus of this book is on the technologies for the transition period, which in the roadmap is characterised by increasing rates of decarbonisation.

The roadmap includes a third category of technologies needed to stabilise $CO_2$ emissions around a new, very low-carbon baseline. Technologies in this category are artificial photosynthesis, high-temperature superconductors, fusion and small-scale nuclear reactors based on particle accelerator technology. Development of these technologies is a high-risk undertaking, which needs public R&D. Experience curves may be useful in assessing the prospects of commercial viability.

# Inside the Learning System I: Technology Structural Change

An important question is how an R&D breakthrough, a major technical change or shift in production process may appear in the experience curve. Examples may be a breakthrough in the production of thin-film photovoltaics or the shift to new temperature-resistant materials for gas turbines. We will refer to these types of changes as *technology structural changes*. The name emphasises that there has been a radical change in the content of the development process, e.g., a shift in the technology paradigm leading to a new variant of the technology or a major change in the way the technology is produced. The change represents a stepwise shift of the technological frontier, and is expected to signal an increased learning rate in the experience curve for technology *costs*.

Experience curves usually measure changes in prices, and there is a risk that the effect of technology structural changes is masked by changes in the market. The first case study presented in Chapter 3 provides an experience curve based on *costs*, which makes it possible to identify the effects of a technology structural change.

The hypothesis is that technology structural changes show up as discontinuities in the experience curve, as specified in Figure 2.4. The discontinuity is in the form of a double knee, a step in the experience curve, indicating a change in the entry point and possibly also in the progress ratio before and after the change. Before the transition period, technology variant A is deployed, but during the transition period investors realise the advantages of variant B. The two variants are assumed to be similar, so that during the transition period variant B can accumulate the experience learned from deploying variant A.

**Figure 2.4. Technology Structural Change**

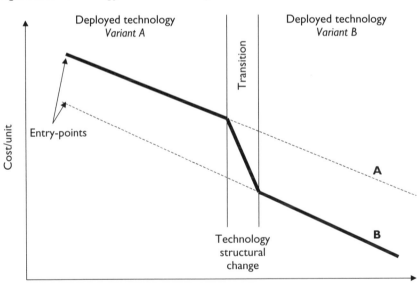

The heavy line is the expected behaviour of the experience curve during a shift of technology from variant A to variant B.

# Outside the Learning System:
# Market Structural Change

The policy analyst will probably have to rely on price rather than cost data when he measures the experience effect. The price experience curve is coupled to the cost experience curve, but it also reflects the sales and pricing strategies of the producers, the investors' bargaining power, and market reactions to public deployment policies.

The Boston Consulting Group (1968) has analysed the relationship between price and cost experience curves, and the following discussion draws on their conclusion. Figure 2.5 shows a complete price-cost cycle for the market introduction of a new product.

The cycle for a viable technology has four phases. In the Development phase, the initial producer sets prices below cost to establish the market. Generally, the initial producer maintains some degree of

Figure 2.5. Price-cost Relations for a New Product

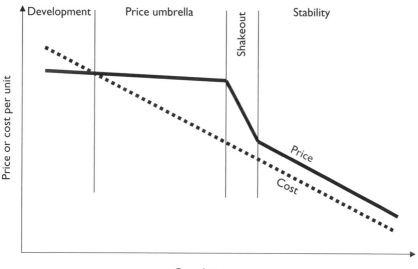

Boston Consulting Group, 1968.

market power as his cost becomes lower than price. As a market leader, he may maintain prices and hold a Price Umbrella over the higher cost producers that are entering the market. In effect, he is then cashing in on his development by trading future market share for current profits. The typical progress ratio for this phase is 90% or more.

Under the Price Umbrella, the new producers will learn and thereby reduce their cost. This leads to an unstable situation, where more producers become low-cost producers and the difference between the price and the cost for these producers becomes larger and larger. The market enters the Shakeout phase when prices fall faster than cost. The Boston Consulting Group (1968) finds progress ratios typically around 60% for this phase, but there are considerable variations around this value. The Shakeout progress ratios are not sustainable, however, because they would bring prices below cost. In the last phase, prices stabilise around an experience curve with the same progress ratio as the cost curve. Stability entails a fixed cost/price ratio.

The price progress ratio in a stable market is thus equivalent to the cost progress ratio. It may be difficult, however, to obtain measurement series long enough to ensure that stable conditions have been reached. The model for the price-cost cycle does provide guidance for determining cost progress ratios from shorter series. The average price progress ratio over one cycle also provides information on the cost progress ratio.

The analysis indicates that the two discontinuities at the start and end of the Shakeout phase signal changes in market structure. Parallel to *technology* structural change, which can be observed from the *cost* experience curve, *market* structural change can be observed from the *price* experience curve. The two are quite distinct phenomena, because a market structural change will have no effect on the cost curve. However, cost curves are difficult to measure, which may tempt the analyst to use the price curve as an indicator for technology structural change. This should be avoided because from a knee in the price curve no conclusion can be drawn about the behaviour of the cost curve.

Figures 2.6-2.8 show experience curves for three energy technologies, which all demonstrate market structural change, although the technologies are in different phases of the cost-price cycle.

**Figure 2.6. Natural Gas Combined Cycle, 1981-1997**

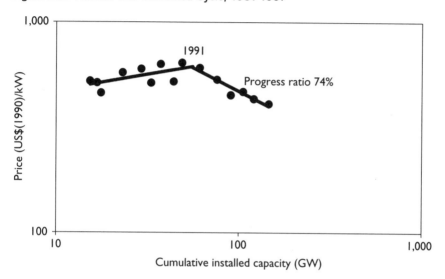

Experience curve for natural gas combined cycle. Prices are for NGCC plants installed in Europe and the NAFTA area. From Claeson (1999).

The market for natural gas combined cycle (NGCC) is in the latter part of a shakeout phase. The experience curve in Figure 2.6 is compiled from information on investments in NGCC projects found in professional journals. The data before 1991 show the scatter typical for information based on a few individual projects. The progress ratio for the period after 1991, however, is based on averages over many projects. Prices before 1991 were rising providing the first market entrants with opportunities to recover development costs. The price situation before 1991 reflected the market power of the first producers but also increased customer valuation of the product due to increased technical performance, e.g., fuel efficiency and reliability. The progress ratio for the shakeout is fairly high, which indicates that the underlying cost experience curve has a progress ratio around 90%, rather than 80%.

Capital costs only account for 20-25% of the total costs of producing electricity from NGCC plants. The dramatic shape of the experience curve for investments in NGCC is therefore not reflected in the experience curve for electricity generated from NGCC in Figure 1.5. Improvements in fuel efficiency during the 1980s compensated for the increase in capital costs for the projects over this period.[10]

More detailed studies of the market for photovoltaic modules reveal structural changes, which do not appear in the analysis of Williams and Terzian (1993), discussed in the previous chapter. Figure 2.7 shows the experience curve based on price series for crystalline silicone. The shakeout period is short and steep. The stability phase has a progress ratio of 79%, which indicates somewhat better prospects for PV than the results obtained by Williams and Terzian which were based on data from the period 1976-1992. In the period 1976-1996, there were changes in the production process so one can not rule out that technology structural changes contributed to the changing shape of the price experience curve.

The experience curve in Figure 2.8 for subsidised Brazilian ethanol shows the typical pattern for the price-cost cycle. During the period 1978-1986, the progress ratio remained at 90%, which the Boston Consulting Group found typical for the umbrella phase. The start of the 1987-1990 shakeout coincides with falling oil prices and the exploitation of Brazilian offshore oil. The progress ratio for the

---

10. Assuming global learning not only for construction of NGCC but also for production of electricity from them gives a progress ratio for electricity production from NGCC of 90% (Claeson, 1999). The EU has increased its share of world NGCC capacity during the 1990s. While the world cumulative production of electricity from NGCC increased by a factor of 3 from 1990 to 1996, the corresponding factor within the EU was 14. Using electricity produced within the EU as a basis for the experience curve as in Figure 1.5 gives then a much higher value for the progress ratio, namely 96%. Using regional cumulative outputs as in Figure 1.5 is legitimate to present and analyse historical developments within a single region. However, whenever experience curves are used for benchmarking, for predictions or for *scenario analysis* it is obviously very important to use cumulative global outputs if the learning is global and regional cumulative outputs if the learning is regional. See also the footnote on photovoltaics for Figure 1.5.

## Figure 2.7. Market Changes for PV Modules, 1976-1996

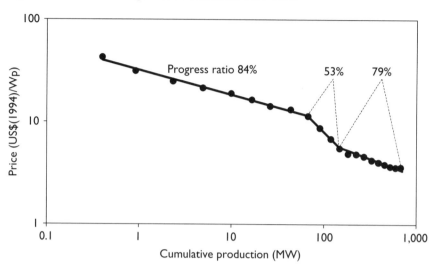

Experience curve showing market structural changes for photovoltaic modules. Data from the EU-ATLAS project and Nitsch (1998).

## Figure 2.8. Brasilian Ethanol, 1978-1995

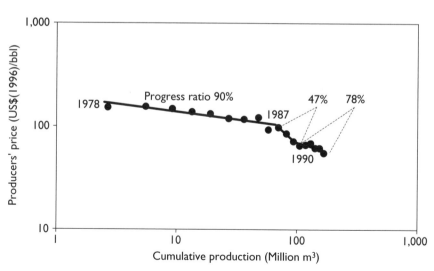

Experience curve for production of ethanol in Brazil. Data from Goldemberg (1996).

stabilisation period after 1990 is still uncertain, but it is consistent with a cost experience curve with about an 80% progress ratio. The average progress ratio for the period 1978-1996 is 80%.

# Inside the Learning System II: Compound Systems

A learning system can exist on many levels. Each learning system is characterised by experience curves, and the experience curves for the larger system depend on the curves for the systems it contains. The experience effect is thus a *recursive* phenomenon. The analyst must choose at what level he will undertake his analysis.

The public policy analyst wants to understand the consequences of experience curves for the energy system and use them to design better policy. In many cases his purpose is well served by remaining at the industrial level, considering only the output of the complete technology without attempting to break the learning system down into production steps or branches.

There are situations, however, when it may be necessary to look at the learning system as a compound system consisting of two or more learning subsystems. One example is the design of deployment policies for photovoltaic systems. Such systems consist of the PV-modules and the so-called balance-of-system (BOS). BOS is equipment which is needed to integrate the modules into the user's system, and it contains different components for remote off-grid applications, building integrated systems or central power systems. The costs for BOS and modules are of the same order of magnitude. The production of BOS and the production of modules are parallel subsystems, which interact to form the output from the total learning system. The learning patterns for BOS and modules are quite different. This means not only that they may have different progress ratios and points of entry, but also that the basis for learning may be different, which is reflected in the way the cumulative output is calculated for the subsystems. The learning for modules is global, so performance should be measured against global production, while the learning for BOS may have elements which cannot be transferred between countries or regions. The different learning patterns of the two subsystems require the policy analyst to treat them separately.

Production of electricity from specific technologies is another example where the policy analyst may find it useful to distinguish learning at different steps in the production chain. The subsystems are in this case arranged in series from production of equipment, siting and construction to generation of electricity.

Figure 2.9 illustrates the US learning system for production of electricity from wind. Each system has a learning loop and its dynamic performance can be characterised by an experience curve. However, the two systems are bound together not only through an output-input relation, but also through informational feed-forward and feed-backward loops. Information on the design of a new turbine is an

**Figure 2.9. US Learning System for Production of Electricity from Wind**

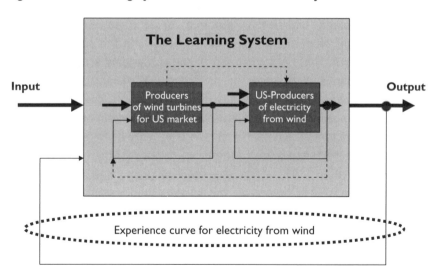

The system contains two subsystems, one producing wind turbines and one producing electricity from wind with the help of wind turbines. The dashed lines represents information feed-forward or feed-backward between the two subsystems.

example of information passed through the feed-forward loop. Conversely, the turbine producers obtain information about effects of different sites and tower heights. The systems learn from each other.

Learning between subsystems effects the experience curve for the total learning system. This curve is more than just the product of the experience curves for the subsystems, it will also describe the interaction between the two systems. In designing R&D and deployment policies, the policy-maker should attempt to link learning cycles that can enhance learning between subsystems. The US, Germany and Sweden concentrated their RD&D efforts on developing large wind turbines during the end of the 1970s and beginning of the 1980s (Gipe, 1995; Carlman, 1990). These efforts were out of phase with the utility market, which had begun to deploy small turbines. In the Danish wind power programme, however, the two subsystems were linked and helped to create a leading world industry for wind power equipment.

Production of electricity from wind energy showed a progress ratio of 68% in the US in the period of 1985-1994 (Figure 2.10). The learning rate is considerably higher than the rate for wind power in the European Union, where the progress ratio was 82% in the period of 1980-1995 (Figure 1.5). A comparison of the subsystems across the two regions shows differences in production of electricity from windmills. A measure of performance for the electricity production subsystem is the annual capacity factor, which is the quotient of actual generation to potential generation, or $\rho$ = (electricity delivered from the plant) $/$ (8760*rated power). The progress ratio for the capacity factor in the US is 78%, while the corresponding value for the European Union is 94%.[11] However, the curve for the US starts from a lower capacity factor than the curve for the EU, and reaches EU values at the end of the observed period. The observed learning rate for the

---

11. Performance is measured as input/output, so formally the progress ratios refer to the inverse of the annual capacity factor, $1/\rho$. Plotting $1/\rho$ as function of cumulative electricity production provides a learning curve, because the wind turbines are just one of several inputs to the process of producing electricity from wind. Experience curves refer to total inputs measured as total costs.

## Figure 2.10. Electricity from wind Energy in USA, 1985-1994

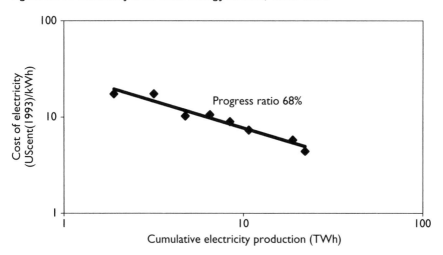

Experience curve for production of electricity from wind energy in USA. US price data are from Kline (1998) and electricity production from Gipe (1995).

US is probably due to a combination of technology and market structural changes. The strong drive for larger turbines during the period improved the annual capacity factor, and the reduction in subsidies led to more careful selection of sites and an effect similar to the shakeout observed for prices.

There are many possible combinations of performance measurements and cumulative outputs. The simple learning model in Figure 2.1 shows that in an experience or learning curve the output to estimate performance and the cumulative output to estimate experience must relate to the same learning system. It may be tempting to relate electricity costs to cumulative installed capacity, which would provide a very steep curve for wind power in the USA with an apparent "progress ratio" of 17%! Figure 2.9 shows that this is relating the performance of the total system to the experience in one of its subsystems. The total system is producing electricity, not wind mills. Strict adherence to the rule of using output from the same learning system is necessary to be able to benchmark results obtained from experience and learning curves.

# CHAPTER 3: MAKING EMERGING TECHNOLOGIES COMMERCIAL

*This chapter demonstrates via three case studies how public policy can be designed to ride the experience curves.*

## Solar Heating – Monitoring and Terminating an RD&D Program

Public RD&D support for a technology or family of technologies usually extends over several years. This raises questions about how to monitor the progress of the research and development and when to terminate the support in order to free resources for new research objects. Support may be ended either because the technology is not advancing or progressing too slowly, or because the technology has reached maturity and further development should be left to the market. In the latter case it may be more correct to say that the technology is docking into the market, rather than breaking even with existing, conventional alternatives.[12] At the *docking point*, the technology may not yet be fully commercial; however, its cost and performance prompt market actors to risk learning investments to bring the technology to commercial status. Public policy may still be necessary to reduce the risk for the market actors, e.g., by internalising environmental cost and creating niche markets, but no targeted public RD&D spending or subsidies for deployment are necessary.

The following case study provides an experience curve analysis of the development of solar heating for swimming pools in Germany. The

---

12. The word "docking" is a space-age metaphor, alluding to the attaching of a space ship to a space station.

federal RD&D programme started in 1975 and ended in 1987, which makes it possible to follow the technology from first experimental installations to commercial deployment. The analysis allows comparison of RD&D support and learning investments and discussions on the support from experience curves in monitoring and terminating RD&D programs. The study relies on analysis performed at the German Bundesminsterium für Bildung, Wissenschaft, Forschung und Technologie.[13]

Figure 3.1 shows German federal spending on energy research, development and demonstration related to swimming pools and sport arenas. The figure also shows the deployment of the solar heating technology, which was supported by the RD&D program. Market penetration indicates that the technology has passed from

**Figure 3.1. Solar Heating Swimming Pools: Germany, 1975-1997**

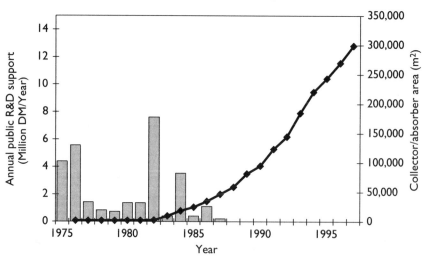

Public RD&D expenditures for solar heated swimming pools in Germany (histogram, left-hand scale) and deployment of the technology measured in installed collector/absorber area (full drawn line, right-hand scale). (Data from Lawitzka, 1992 and 1999)

---

13. See Lawitzka (1992, 1999). Also private communication from H. Lawitzka, Bundesministerium für Wirtschaft und Technologie, Referat 411, Heinemannstrasse 2, D-53175 Bonn (current affiliation).

the development and demonstration stage to the commercial stage. The deployment has sextupled from 1987, when support was terminated, until 1997. But Figure 3.1 also raises several questions regarding the relationship between public RD&D spending and technology performance. What is involved in the take off in 1982? Why terminate the programme in 1987? The experience curve in Figure 3.2 provides a tool for answering these questions.

**Figure 3.2. Solar Heated Swimming Pools, 1975-1993: Experience Curve and RD&D Support**

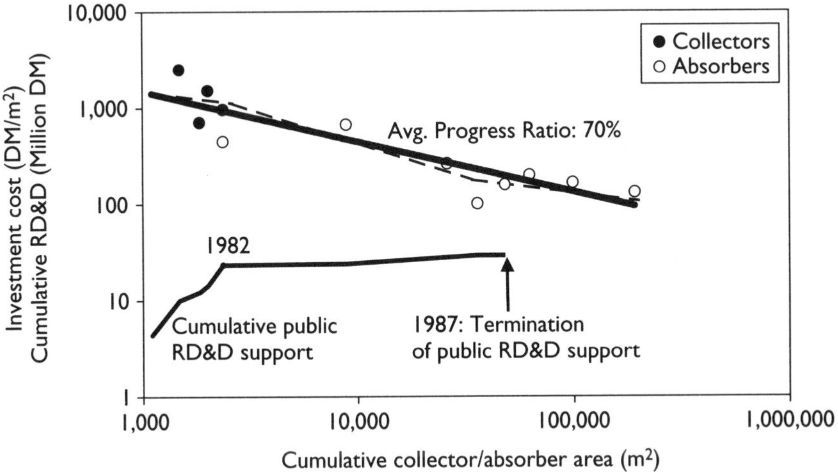

Experience curve for technology to provide solar heated swimming pools and cumulative RD&D expenditures for such technology. The dashed line through the data points shows the expected experience curve during a technology structural change involving a transition from collector to absorber technology. The solid line represents the fit of a single power function to all data points and indicates an average progress ratio of 70% for the period 1975-1993. The $R^2$-value for the solid line is 0.80. (Data from Lawitzka, 1992, 1998)

The learning system for solar heated swimming pools consists of two competing technologies for capturing solar energy: collector and absorber systems. In the terminology suggested in chapter 2, we have a compound learning system with two competing, parallel subsystems. The winning technology cannot be picked at the start of the process, but emerges from the learning process itself. For the public decision maker, technology learning supported by public spending includes understanding limitations and exploiting advantages of the two technologies. As the limitations of the initially promising collector technology became apparent in the beginning of the 1980s, projects switched from collector to absorber technology, generating a structural change in the learning system.

The dashed line in Figure 3.2 is based on our analysis of technology structural change in Chapter 2, and indicates the expected shape of the experience curve for a system that switches from collector to absorber technology. The start of the transition period was 1982. The cost data show the scatter typical for measurements based on individual projects, and therefore only permit placing the end of the transition period in the period of 1985-1987. For the separate collector and absorber technologies we have assumed the standard progress ratios of 82%.[14] Within the transition period the progress ratio was 55-60%, implying that investments cost were reduced by 40% or more for each doubling of accumulated installed area. Such a high learning rate indicates an efficient transition from collector to absorber technology.

The dashed line in Figure 3.2 provides a qualitative understanding of the learning process, but has large numerical uncertainties. For a quantitative analysis, we will rely on the solid line, which represents an average experience curve for the period of 1975-1993. The average progress ratio for this period is 70%.

Figure 3.2 also shows the cumulative federal RD&D spending as a function of cumulative collector and absorber area. The research and development programme was built up in the period of 1975-1982, when 80% of the federal RD&D was disbursed. When RD&D support was terminated in 1987, ten installations had been built with federal support. The investment costs for the last installations were

---

14. Nitsch (1998) finds a progress ratio of 84% for all types of collector installations in Germany from 1985 to 1997. The standard progress ratio of 82% therefore seems a good working assumption for each of the two individual solar technologies for swimming pools.

100-200 DM/m$^2$, compared with costs of 3000 DM/m$^2$ when the programme started in 1975. Public RD&D was a primary agent in reducing investment costs by one order of magnitude. At the start of the transition period in 1982, the cumulative public learning investments sent the technology down the experience curve resulting in the take-off for solar heated swimming pools seen in Figure 3.1. From the successful marketing of the technology over the last ten years, we also conclude that the investment cost reached in 1987 provided a good docking point for commercial interests.

A comparison between federal RD&D spending and learning investments illustrates how public spending seeds the development process. Table 3.1 shows expenditures during three different phases of the ride down the experience curve: from 1975 until RD&D support peaked out in 1982

Table 3.1. Learning Investments and Federal RD&D Support for Solar Heated Swimming Pools

| Period | Federal RD&D Support (million DM) | Deployment | |
|---|---|---|---|
| | | Learning Investments (million DM) | Total Investments (million DM) |
| RD&D build up: 1975-1982 | 23 | 4 | 5 |
| Take-off: 1983-1987 | 6 | 8 | 15 |
| Commercialisation: 1988-1990 | 0 | 1 | 6 |
| After break-even: 1991-1997 | – | – | (25)* |
| Total: 1975-1997 | 29 | 13 | (51) |

* Estimated assuming 82% progress ratio after break even.

("RD&D build up"), from 1983 until the docking point in 1987 ("take-off") and from 1988 until break-even around 1990 ("commercialisation"). At the break-even point, the technology successfully competed with conventional heating alternatives, such as light fuel oil.[15] For comparison, the table also shows the total investments in solar heated swimming pools. The difference between total and learning investments is the corresponding cost for a conventional alternative for heating.

Public RD&D spending dominated the build-up phase. Public funds provided most of the learning investments for the deployment of the technology, but the major part of the funds supported activities necessary to initiate and feed the development process. Examples of such activities are build-up of competence and search for new knowledge within research organisations, and measurement and evaluation programmes around the pilot installations.

Learning investments are still larger than the cost for a conventional alternative during the take-off phase. Most of these investments are financed through public funds. Finally, in the commercialisation phase, learning investments are only a small part in the total investments and are provided by the implementers.

Table 3.1 shows that public RD&D spending was twice the total learning investments. There are several reasons for the dominance of public spending in this case. The build-up phase coincides with the start of the large-scale public energy RD&D programme after the 1973 oil crisis. The relationship between public RD&D spending and total learning cost therefore reflects the large entry cost for this programme. The switch from collector to absorber technology shortened the take-off and commercialisation phases, reducing the demands for learning investments. However, in spite of the favourable learning situation, these investments still represented 25% of the total investments until 1997.

---

15. For calculating the learning investments in Table 3.1, the break-even point is set by the short range marginal cost (SRMC) of light fuel oil. Taxes are included. For the period of 1988-1993 the average SRMC for deliveries to households and industry is 5 pf/kWh, corresponding to an investment cost of about 150 DM/m$^2$.

Table 3.1 signals the need for market learning to follow the RD&D build up. The purpose of this learning is to bring prices to competitive levels. In the case of solar heated swimming pools public RD&D expenditures and learning investments are strongly inter-related.

A decision-maker at the end of the build-up or take-off phases does not have access to the information in Figures 3.1 and 3.2. How can he use the experience curve phenomenon to assess the prospects or success of the program, and decide if support should be continued or terminated?

The decision-maker at the end of the build-up phase could use the standard value of 82% for the progress ratio and the experience gathered until 1982 to fit an entry point for the experience curve. His assessment of the future prospects of the programme will then completely depend on the importance he gives to the information from the new installations using absorber technology, that is whether or not he realises that he is on the brink of a technology structural change. Treating all information equal, and fitting an 82% experience curve to all available information without discriminating between collector and absorber installations, would place break-even at several million square meters with learning investments of 100-200 million DM. In hindsight, such an analysis would have lead to wrong conclusions and might have forced termination of an otherwise successful programme.

However, the decision-maker can also conclude that absorber technology is more viable. He can then estimate break-even and remaining learning investments in two ways, which reflect different assumptions on the length of the transition period. Assuming a very short transition period, he can rely exclusively on the available results from the absorber installations and estimate an experience curve for this technology assuming a 82% progress ratio. This provides an optimistic estimate for learning investments. Another method is to use all available data, and let these define the starting point for a more extended transition period. Experiences from similar situations indicate, that it should be possible to achieve a 70% progress ratio during the transition period. In hindsight, 70% turns out to be a conservative estimate considering that the *ex post* analysis above indicates a progress ratio of 60% or less for the transition period. Both methods will yield break-even around 100,000 m$^2$ and remaining learning investments from 6 to 10 million DM. From our viewpoint in 1998, we observe, that these 1982 estimates bracket the values found in our *ex post* analysis. The 1982 decision-maker concludes, that success is within sight and the remaining learning investments are less than the RD&D money already spent on the project. The analysis favours a continuation of the programme.

In 1987, the analyst will have learnt more about the progress ratio for the learning system. The decision-maker can obtain information about remaining learning investments, in order to support his decision on a docking point. In hindsight, the data will tend to underestimate the learning investments to be paid by the market actors, but will also supply an upper limit of 1 million DM for these investments, which is the value obtained in our *ex post* analysis in Table 3.1. This means that the share of learning investments in the total investments necessary to reach the break-even point is estimated to be less than 20%. The decision on the docking point will depend on how the decision-maker assesses the willingness of the market actors to supply the remaining learning investments.

The case study shows that experience curves provide a systematic framework for collecting and assessing information and for weighing arguments for and against continuation of public RD&D support. Like all management tools, they have to be used with prudence and corroborated with other information. Our experiment with virtual decision makers in 1982 and 1987 shows that experience curves will not substitute for the good judgement of the decision maker, but that they will widen and sharpen his vision.

## Windpower – Deployment Support to Increase Learning Investments

Commercialisation of wind power requires much larger efforts than those needed to bring solar heating for swimming pools to the docking point. The previous case study described a well defined programme lasting one decade from start to finish, and where the effect of RD&D support could be followed on a project by project basis. Public RD&D projects for wind power have generated important insights into the technology, but the reductions in investment costs have come through large-scale deployment involving many actors in the energy system. Learning has been a diffused phenomenon, occurring at several stages in the implementation process and in several different countries with large-scale deployment. In this case, the public decision-maker cannot monitor the effect of deployment programmes on individual projects, but instead has to design the support to stimulate learning investments from many sources and find ways to evaluate the efficiency of his intervention in the marketplace.

In spite of the large difference between the wind power and the solar heating programmes, we can use the same methodology in analysing the policy measures. The purpose of the analysis is to see how efficient the measures have been in stimulating learning investments.

Figure 3.3 indicates the scope of technology learning involved in bringing electricity from wind to break even with electricity from fossil fuels. The figure shows experience curves for wind electricity in the EU for the installations with the highest and the lowest costs. The best wind power plants produced electricity at a price competitive with electricity from coal-fired power plants in 1995. The learning investments until 1995 were about 3 billion ECU and commercialisation of wind power for high cost plants will require another 2-3 billion ECU.[16]

Most of the learning investments in the EU have been made in Germany, Denmark, the UK and the Netherlands. During the 1990s, Germany dominated the market and this case study focuses on the German wind power experience. Figure 3.3 shows the experience curve for a compound system consisting of turbine manufacturing, siting, construction and operation of wind power plants as discussed in section 2.4. The following case study relies on a recent measurement

---

16. Historical learning investments in the EU are estimated for the average wind power technology assuming that the technical lifetime of a wind power plant is 15 years.

**Figure 3.3. Electricity from Wind Energy in EU, 1980-1995**

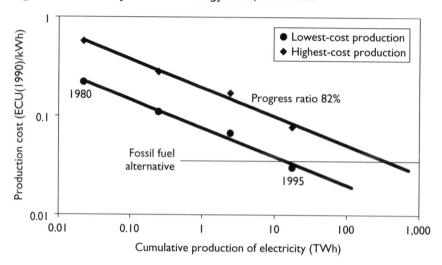

Spread in the cost of producing electricity from wind energy. Experience curves for plants with the highest and lowest production costs during the year of their installation. Data from the EU ATLAS project (Marsh, 1998).

of the experience curve for wind turbines (Durstewitz and Hoppe-Kilpper, 1999) and confines the analysis to turbine manufacturing. The output of the learning system therefore consists of all turbines sold in Germany from 1990 to 1998. As more measurements become available, the analysis can be extended to siting, construction and operation.

Wind power capacity increased from 60 to 2900 MW in Germany from 1990 to 1998. The experience curve in Figure 3.4 shows that this reduced prices for the wind turbines from 2500 to 1700 DM (1995)/kW. The progress ratio of 92% is smaller than the ratio for wind turbines from Danish manufacturers, indicating that the learning rate is twice as large in Germany as in Denmark (see Figure 1.2 in Chapter 1). Figure 3.5 shows a strong drive towards larger plants on the German market. This suggests that the apparent higher learning rate in Germany reflects the fact that larger units have smaller specific costs. However, economies of scale only explain a small part of the

Figure 3.4. Wind Turbines in Germany, 1990-1998

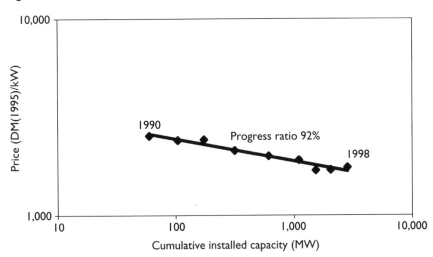

Experience curves for wind turbines sold in Germany 1990-1998. Prices are averages over annually installed capacity of wind turbines of different sizes and different manufacturers. (Adopted from Durstewitz and Hoppe-Kilpper, 1999.)

Figure 3.5. Average Capacity of Wind Turbine Units Installed Each Year

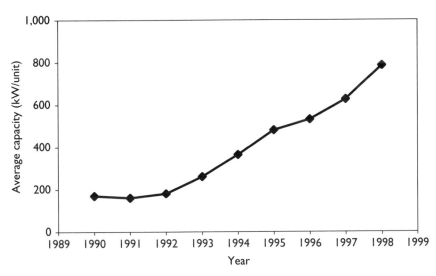

(Data courtesy of Durstewitz, 1999)

difference. More detailed studies reveal that over 50% of the installed units consist of 500/600 kW turbines. List prices for turbines in this class show a progress ratio of 93%, indicating that the observed progress ratio is in fact driven by price reductions by the manufacturers. A possible explanation for the learning rate is technology spill-over, i.e., Germany has imported experience, for instance from Denmark. In case of spill-over, the higher learning rate is not sustainable and cannot be used to predict future prices. Investigation of the spill-over effect is of great interest, but requires comprehensive global and cross-countries studies of turbine markets. The following analysis will only use the experience curve in Figure 3.4 to estimate learning investments until 1998, which means that the experience curve is used not to predict future investment prices but to reconstruct a historical development.

In the period of 1990-1998, the German market for wind turbines grew by an average of 40% per year from 41 MW installed per year to 800 MW installed per year. Federal programmes supported this growth.

Before 1989, there was no real market for wind turbines in Germany. At that time, the Federal Ministry for Science, Education, Research and Technology (BMBF) announced the "100 MW Wind Programme". In 1989 and 1990, an operator of a wind power plant could receive 0.08 DM/kWh from this programme and 0.09 DM/kWh from the utility for electricity delivered to the grid. Investment subsidies were given at the start of the programme and there were additional grants offered by the Federal States (Länder). The "Electricity Feed Law" (EFL) which came into effect January 1991 further benefited the use of wind power. The EFL stipulated that the utilities had to pay the operator 90% of the average tariffs for the final consumer. For 1999 this amounted to 0.1652 DM/kWh. The "100 MW program" was enlarged to a "250 MW program" in 1991. Within this program, the subsidy for the operator is either 0.06 or 0.08 DM/kWh, depending on whether the electricity is fed into the grid or is used by the operator himself. Subsidies can only be received for a maximum of ten years, and the total amount of the subsidy must not exceed 25%

of the cost for wind turbine, site preparations and constructions (Bundesanzeiger, 1994).[17]

The federal programmes stimulated further activities outside the programmes. Figure 3.6 shows the ratio of cumulative capacity of all wind turbines in Germany versus the ones supported by the federal programmes. There is a clear take-off for external activities around 1993. Out of 500 MW coming into operation in 1996 only 20 MW was subsidised by the 250 MW program. From 1993 to 1997, the market expanded strongly which brought more suppliers to the market. Most of the expansion took place outside the 100/250 MW programme.

**Figure 3.6. Changing Markets for Wind Turbines in Germany**

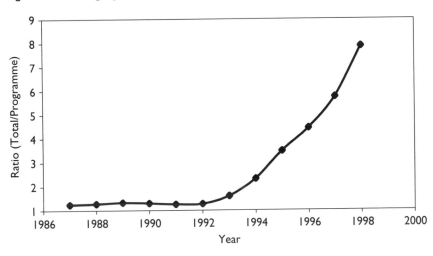

The curve shows the ratio between total cumulative capacity and cumulative capacity in federal programmes. (Adopted from Stump, 1997; data for 1997 and 1998 from Durstewitz, 1999).

---

17. The subsidy is for investments in the turbine and in constructions at the site, although payment of the subsidy is based on operational performance. The better the installation performs the faster the investor can claim the subsidy. The basis for calculating the subsidy includes the costs for the wind turbine including transport, commissioning, tower construction, access roads, building permit, and site relevant planning (e.g., wind measurements). Private persons, non-commercial organisations and farmers could opt for direct, one-time investment subsidies, which were based on technical properties of the wind power installation. This option was of interest for smaller turbines and mostly applied to installations early in the programme. Less than 10% of the total installed 361 MW in the 100/250 MW programme received direct investment subsidies (Windheim, 1999).

The Electricity Feed Law probably explains a major part of the take-off in wind turbine installations. The law reduced the uncertainty for the investors, because it guaranteed a price for electricity produced from the wind turbine. This price lies considerably above the cost for producing electricity from technologies which the market currently considers cost-efficient. The difference reimburses the investor for his contribution to the learning investments for the wind technology. With the EFL in place, the investor thus makes a learning investment relying on refunds from the utilities and in the end from the electricity consumer. However, EFL in its present form does not allow for the experience effect. The guaranteed price is fixed to the average tariffs for the final consumer, but the experience effect implies that it should be progressively reduced for future investors as both manufacturers and producers proceed down their experience curves.[18]

EFL provides a general stimulation of deployment and learning investments through administrative policy measures. The 100/250 MW Wind Programme represents more targeted measures based on government subsidies to develop the market for wind power plants. An interesting question is the cost-efficiency of this programme from a public policy viewpoint. An analysis based on the experience curve in Figure 3.4 and on learning investments provides a first indication of the programme's efficiency.

After 1997, no more plants were accepted into the 100/250 MW Wind Programme, but plants in the programme continued to receive subsidies for their operation.[19] The programme thus recognised the basic message from experience curve analysis. Subsidies for market-induced technology development should be limited in time and geared to initiate or accelerate the ride down the experience curve

---

18. In February 2000, the German Bundestag passed a new law on priority for renewable energy. This new law supersedes EFL and allows for the experience effect

19. 31 December 1995 marked the deadline for proposals in the 250 MW programme. Grants were authorised for this last round of proposals during 1996 and 1997, and the investor then regularly had 18 months to build and achieve commissioning of the plant.

towards break-even. The subsidies should cease when the technology has docked with the commercial market. The experience curve also suggests that an efficient programme should reduce subsidies as prices fall, giving larger subsidies to early investors, who bear the burden of higher learning investments than later entrants. The 25% rule in the 250 MW Wind Programme relates the subsidies to actual prices, and therefore allows for the experience effect. However, basing subsidies on total cost rather than learning investments may still favour the late entrant and may subsidise his commercial investments. This risk is reduced through the criteria for acceptance into the programme (Bundesanzeiger, 1994). These criteria refer to the technological maturity of a turbine type and to the need for demonstration of different sites and installations, which made it possible for the funding agency to direct subsidies to those installations and sites where learning opportunities were most needed. The plants in the 250 MW Wind Programme can therefore act as forerunners, which stimulate further learning investments outside the programme. The following analysis assumes that all subsidies lead to learning investments.

A first indication of how efficient the programme has been in stimulating learning investments is provided by the ratio of the total learning investments made by all investors to the subsidies provided by the government programme. A ratio of one means that government subsidies are funding all learning investments; a ratio larger than one indicates additional contributions from market actors, e.g. utilities, private investors and, in the end, electricity consumers. A ratio less than one signals that the government may be paying for investments that should be assumed by market participants.

The experience curve in Figure 3.4 shows the market *price* of wind turbines, and from this curve the learning investments made by the *investors* can be calculated. The curve is smooth without discontinuities which indicates that the German turbine market has been stable during the observed period. On a *stable* market there is very little difference between the learning investments paid by the investor and the learning investments made by the manufacturer.[20] This means that we can rely on the *price* experience curve measured on the market to calculate learning investments and study development costs, without discussing financial strategies among the manufacturers.

Learning investments refer to costs above the corresponding cost for the presently cost-efficient market alternatives. With the present price for wind turbines, the best wind power plants can compete with conventional technologies (Marsh, 1998). The following estimates of learning investments use a break-even price of 1600 DM (1995)/kW.

Figure 3.7 compares the learning investments in wind turbines to the annual public expenditures for wind RD&D from 1977 to 1998 and for the 100/250 MW Wind Programme from 1989 with a forecast until 2005. The annual learning investments peak in 1994 and will be zero after 2000, following our assumptions on break-even price and continuing high rates of deployment. RD&D expenditures peak around 1980 due to RD&D projects on large wind turbines, and then slowly decrease. Expenditures in the 100/250 MW Wind Programme peak in 1996 and terminate about ten years later, when the final operational subsidies for the last installations allowed into the programme are paid out.

The total government subsidies for the 100/250 MW programme are 330 million DM (1995). The subsidies include the costs for site preparations and installations, which should be deducted before calculating the ratio of learning investments to subsidies for the wind turbines. For German plants, Kleinkauf et al. (1997) find that the cost of the wind turbine is 67-73% of the total investment costs. This is in

---

20. According to our discussion in Section 2.4 based on the findings of the Boston Consulting Group (1968), the ratio between cost and price is constant in a stable market. In Figure 3.4, the cost curve will be a straight line parallel and below the price line, i.e., it will have the same progress ratio of 92%. For instance, an 8% price margin is equal to a price/cost ratio of 1.08, which gives the (average) manufacturer about 25% return on equity. Changing the price margin, will change the total investments but leave the estimates of learning investments practically unaffected. The reason is that the change in price margin will, for the manufacturer, change the comparative cost of the cost-efficient market alternative by the same factor. A stable market thus provides only a very small premium to the developer. The conclusion is that we can use the price experience curve and the concept of learning investments to study development cost without discussing financial strategies among the manufacturers.

## Figure 3.7. Learning Investments and Governments Expenditures

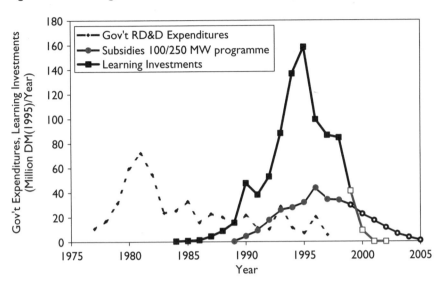

Total learning investments by all investors in wind turbines and federal government expenditures for wind energy. "Gov't RD&D expenditures" are expenditures for RD&D on wind energy outside the 100/250 MW programme. Open circles and squares are forecasts. Note that subsidies are paid out on the basis of electricity production during a maximum period of ten years after the investment. Subsidies are therefore paid out until the middle of next decade, although the 250 MW programme effectively ceased in 1996. (RD&D expenditures are calculated from IEA Statistics. Information about the 100/250 MW programme are from Windheim, 1999).

agreement with estimates of 68-73% for installations in Denmark and California (Gipe, 1995). However, the basis for the subsidies does not include the cost for connection to the grid, which amounts to 8-10% of total costs. We therefore assume that 80% or 260 million DM (1995) of the subsidies supports the purchase of wind turbines. The total learning investments for turbines from the start of the 100/250 MW programme is 810 million DM (1995). The ratio of learning investments to subsidies is thus 3.1, meaning that for each DM spent by the government the market actors have provided 2.1 DM.

The estimate of learning investments depends on the break-even point. Using 1450 DM (1995)/kW as the price at break-even will increase the learning investments until 1998 to 1230 million DM (1995), leading to a ratio between total learning investments and subsidies of 4.7. Lowering the break-even price thus increases the leverage of the 100/250 MW Wind Programme.[21]

In 1998, the ratio of total wind power capacity and cumulative installed capacity in the federal programme was 7.9 (see Figure 3.6). This ratio is considerably larger than the ratio between total learning investments and subsidies. The difference between the two ratios implies that the share of learning investments relative to the total investments is larger for plants inside the programme than for the average wind energy turbine. This suggests that the 100/250 MW Wind programme has been successful in directing subsidies towards those new turbines where the need for learning investments was the largest.

The analysis of learning investments thus indicates that the 100/250 MW Wind Programme achieved two purposes. It stimulated learning investments outside of the programme, while keeping the share of learning investments for plants within the programme larger than for plants outside the programme. Both achievements contributed to the development of a market for wind power plants in Germany. The 100/250 MW Wind Programme was cost-efficient from the public spending viewpoint. The Electricity Feed Law cannot be analysed in the same way as the 100/250 Wind Programme. Studies of EFL have to look at learning obtained by the producer of electricity from wind, which requires time series of electricity production cost from wind turbines. Such time series are still not available.

---

21. One could argue that learning investments should be calculated from an increasing break-even price for wind turbines between 1989 and 1998 since improved load factors and reduced operations and maintenance costs (O&M) have increased the price at which wind turbines become cost-efficient alternatives. For instance, in 1990 the cost of a turbine needed to be less than 700 DM (1995)/kW in order to make wind energy cost-efficient, while cost-efficiency required turbine costs around 1400 DM (1995)/kW in 1998. However, the argument confuses learning in two different systems. Increasing load factors and decreasing O&M costs are the result of learning within the electricity production system, which spills over to the manufacturing system. The break-even price for the manufacturing system is thus calculated using the load factor and O&M costs at the break-even point (see footnote 2 in Chapter 1). The break-even point represents the intercept between the experience curve for wind turbines and the curve for the increasing cost-efficient price. Extrapolating information on load factors and O&M costs (Marsh, 1998; ISET, 1999) put the break-even point around 5000 MW cumulative installed capacity at a price of 1600 DM (1995)/kW. A break-even price of 1450 DM (1995)/kW assumes that there will be only small improvements in load factors and O&M costs after 1998.

The pattern that emerges from Figure 3.7 is similar to the one for solar heated swimming pools; an initial period of large public RD&D spending is followed by a period dominated by learning investments with large-scale applications of the technology. This pattern is expected based on the two-pronged policy for technology learning in section 2.2. The periods are longer and more distinct for wind power than for solar heated swimming pools, and a clearly defined deployment programme marked the beginning of the learning phase for wind power turbines.

Government support and learning investments were more than one order of magnitude larger for wind power than for solar heating. The experience curves for the two technologies explain this difference. Wind power had a favourable initial position, because the cost at the entry point was only twice the cost at break-even, while the entry cost for solar heated swimming pools was more than ten times larger than the break-even cost. The ratios of learning investments over total investments reflect the different entry costs. For the period of 1984-1998, learning investments for wind turbines were only 12% of the total investments shown in Figure 3.8, while they absorbed 50% of the total investments during the learning phase for solar heated swimming

**Figure 3.8. Investments in Wind Turbines in Germany**

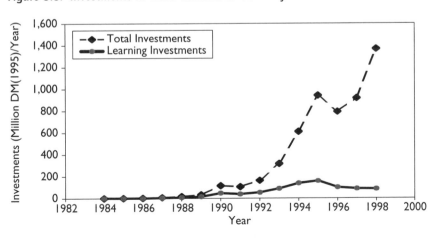

Total investments and learning investments for wind turbines in Germany.

pools (see Table 3.1). However, the advantage in entry cost does not compensate for the huge difference in learning rates; i.e., 30% (=100-70) for solar heated swimming pools but only 8% (=100-92) for wind turbines. To reduce prices by 50% required a fourfold increase in cumulative installed capacity for the solar technology. The same price reduction for wind turbines required an increase in cumulative installed capacity by a factor of 256![22] It is thus the high progress ratio for wind turbines which generates the need for large learning investments.

The wind energy case shows how experience curves can be used for *ex-post* evaluation of policy measures. Experience curves can also be developed into tools for previewing and monitoring the effects of policy measures. The experience curve provides an analytical tool to evaluate and compare policy measures in different countries. Such a "second order learning" is needed to manage the ride down the experience curve for the next generation of $CO_2$-friendly technologies, such as photovoltaics or fuel cells. These technologies have initial costs which are 10-50 times higher than break-even costs. Presently measured or inferred progress ratios indicate values around 80%. Technology structural change may appear as in the case for solar heated swimming pools, but cannot be assumed in the planning phase. The learning investments are therefore expected to be orders of magnitude larger than for wind energy, which increases the need to optimise public policy measures to support deployment. The next case study deals with photovoltaics and how experience curves can be used to design and monitor policy measures.

## Photovoltaics – Creating and Supporting New Niche Markets

To create a viable commercial market for wind power requires learning investments of a few billion US$. For renewable technologies, such as photovoltaics, which could potentially provide large reductions in $CO_2$-

---

22. A factor of four is equal to two doublings of cumulative installed capacity, and a price reduction for solar heated swimming pools of $(1- 0.3)^2 = 0.5$. A factor of 256 is equal to 8 doubling times $(256 = 2^8)$ , and a price reduction of $(1- 0.92)^8 = 0.5$. In fact, the German wind power capacity increased by a factor of 380 between 1988 and 1998!

emissions the remaining learning investments are around a hundred billion US$. To accomplish such learning, efforts have to be sustained over several decades. Two conditions must be fulfilled to provide the large amount of learning investments for a single technology. Firstly, government subsidies must find greater multipliers than in the case for wind power, secondly, the learning has to be global.

This case study focuses on the Japanese programme for grid-connected photovoltaics (PV) in residential areas. From the point of view of technology learning, the objective of the programme is to create niche markets, which can grow and ultimately provide learning investments without any need for subsidies. Together, such markets thus provide a docking point for photovoltaic technology in the sense discussed at the beginning of this chapter.

A niche market for PV puts a premium on the specific characteristics of PV technology, e.g., the technology provides a modular, distributed source of electricity, which is applicable on a very small scale, independent of fuels, and free of emissions during operation. PV will have a high value in areas with large cooling demands, where a distributed source of electricity can follow the cooling load and can avoid central production costs to satisfy peak demand and investments to increase distribution capacity. Japanese metropolitan areas have high costs for both peak production and electricity distribution.

Tsuchiya analysed the prospects for Japanese niche markets for photovoltaics in a seminal paper from 1989 (Tsuchiya, 1989). His results are reproduced in Table 3.2 and Figure 3.9 and provide important insights into the way that niche markets can lead to viable projects. The table identifies four different niche markets. The line labelled "Niche Markets" in the figure represents the cumulative demands from these markets. Experience curves are constructed for progress ratios of 70%, 76% and 80%.[23] The cost of electricity production from central fossil fuel power plants is also indicated in the diagram.

---

23. Strictly speaking, the curves 70%, 76% and 80% are not experience curves because the x- and y-axis do not refer to the output from the same learning system (see Chapter 2). Tsuchiya calculated the price of electricity from experience curves for the investment costs of the total system (incl. BOS), assuming a conversion factor of 0.22 (yen/kWh)/(yen/Wp)

## Table 3.2. Niche Markets for Photovoltaics in Japan

| Electricity Supply Cost (Yen/kWh) | | Market (MW) | Cumulative Market (MW) | Application |
|---|---|---|---|---|
| (Interval) | (Average) | | | |
| 90-50 | (75) | 20-40 | 30 | Substitute for Diesel-engine electricity in remote area |
| 28-36 | (34) | 3,600-5,200 | 4,430 | Public Use. Office building. |
| 27-31 | (29) | 17,000-27,000 | 26,440 | Residential use |
| 15-29 | (25) | 10,000-14,000 | 38,440 | Industrial use |

Tsuchiya, 1989.

## Figure 3.9. Docking PV Technology to Niche Markets in Japan

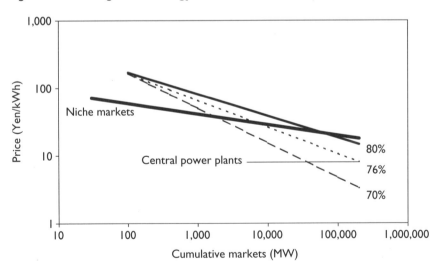

Docking points to Japanese niche markets for photovoltaics assuming experience curves with progress ratios of 80%, 76% and 70%. The line market "Niche Markets" represents a fit to the data in Table 3.2. Adopted from Tsuchiya (1989).

Competition with electricity production in central power stations is the ultimate goal for PV technology. Figure 3.9 indicates that this will require deployment of more than 100 GW of photovoltaics for progress ratios of 76% or more. This is consistent with our previous analysis in Chapter 1. Only with a very optimistic progress ratio of 70% can PV be expected to compete with fossil technologies at less than 100 GW of cumulative sales. There is no indication that such high learning rate can be achieved. The existence of niche markets radically changes the prospects for PV. Tsuchiya's analysis shows that much less deployment is required to produce PV technology at niche market prices. Figure 3.9 places the docking point at 50 GW, 6 GW and 1.4 GW for progress ratios of 80%, 76% and 70%, respectively. After docking into the niche markets, PV technology has access to self-propelling, commercial markets, which will provide the learning investments for the further ride down the experience curve.

Niche markets provide a huge improvement over an approach which relies only on the utility market for conventional electric technology. However, policy measures are needed to start up the niche markets, because the current price of PV is still larger than the willingness to pay in these markets.

Japan's PV-Roof programme started in 1993 and uses subsidies to lower the price for residential, grid-connected PV-systems towards the docking point into the niche markets. Figure 3.10 shows the results from 1993 to 1998 with forecasts through 2000.[24]

The subsidy is installation price less cost paid by the investor, and currently represents half of the difference between the actual installation price and a target price of 3.0 US$/Wp. Since the programme started, the prices for the complete system have fallen from over 30 US$/$W_p$ to about 8 US$/$W_p$ in 1998. Subsidies are reduced as prices fall and will

---

24. Information about installed capacity and prices from 1993 to1998 are from Ikki et al. (1999). Forecasts for 1999 and 2000 are from Kyocera America Inc., published in PV News, Vol.16, No 12, p.3, December 1997. Information about subsidies are from the Japanese Ministry of International Trade and Industry (MITI). Following PV News we use the short-name "PV-Roof Programme". The official name is Residential PV System Dissemination Programme.

Figure 3.10. Japan's PV-Roof Programme: Use of Niche Markets

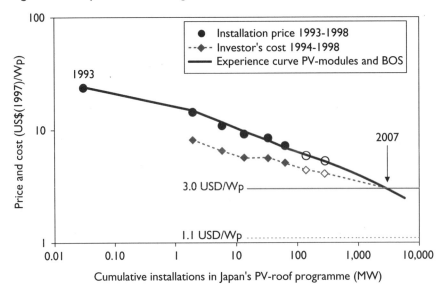

Installation price and investor's cost after subsidies for the PV-system in Japan's PV-Roof programme. Filled points show the actual prices and costs from 1993 to 1998 and open points are forecasts for 1999 and 2000. The full line is a fit to the installation prices with experience curves for PV-modules and Balance-of-System (BOS).

eventually be phased out. A price of 3.0 US$/Wp corresponds to a production cost for electricity of 28 Yen/kWh, which provides the docking into the large niche markets in Table 3.2. The dotted line through investor's cost tracks a segment of the "Niche Markets" curve in Figure 3.9.

The docking point of 3 US$/Wp is supported by evidence form other countries. The Utility Photovoltaic Group (1994) consisting of 81 electric utilities in the US found that a "PV system price of about $3,000/kW emerges as the potential turning point for selfsustaining PV commercialization for domestic markets". However, the niche market curve may be flatter than indicated in Figure 3.10, moving the docking point higher. A tentative, more optimistic target price of 5 US$/$W_p$ is also considered in the PV-Roof programme. Such a docking point would reflect a higher willingness-to-pay among the investors, e.g., due to environmental factors. The basis for the following analysis is the more conservative estimate for the docking point of 3 US$/$W_p$, but 5 US$/$W_p$ will be used to test the sensitivity of the results.

The experience curve gives a qualitative understanding of the price reductions in Japan's PV-Roof programme. However, to set goals and to estimate the costs of these goals require more quantitative analysis. Figure 3.10 therefore also provides a fit of an experience curve to the installation prices with a forecast through 2010. The peculiar shape of the experience curve is the result of two factors:

- *Compound learning system.* The PV-system contains two components that learn at different rates and start with different experiences, namely, the PV-modules and the Balance-of-System (BOS) for a residential, grid-connected installation. The compound experience curve in Figure 3.10 is based on the experience curve for modules on the world market until 1997, which gives a progress ratio of 79% and cumulative sales of 800 MW. For BOS, a progress ratio of 82% is assumed.[25] The cost and cumulative sales of BOS in 1994 are parameters used to fit the compound experience curve to the observed results for the period of 1994-1998.

- *Global learning – local deployment.* The market created by the PV-Roof programme is part of the total world market for PV-modules and for BOS. The success of the programme will therefore depend on the development of markets outside of Japan. The growth rate for the module market outside Japan is assumed to remain at 15% per year, which characterised the market from 1985 to 1995. Residential systems are assumed to be a strongly expanding market

---

25. The assumption reduces prices for BOS by a factor of 4 from 1994 to 2000, and is crucial for fitting the compound experience curve in Figure 3.8 to the observed points. Progress ratio of 82% is consistent with the price series reported by Ikki et al. (1999) and is equal to the most probable value observed by Dutton and Thomas (1984), see Figure 1.3. The integration of PV-systems into materials for roofs and walls and into the architectural design of the building is decisive for further price reductions. Structurally integrated PV-systems are new developments, which open the possibility of a technology structural change in the design of BOS. Such change can lead to a step-wise reduction in BOS price (cf. the first case study and section 2.3), reduce subsidies and learning investments, and move the docking point closer in time.

also outside of Japan. Through year 2000, the growth rate in the Japanese programme is over 70%/year, but after year 2000 the growth rates are assumed to reduce gradually to 15%/year.

Extrapolation of the experience curve until 2010 indicates that if the programme is unchanged PV technology will reach the docking point around 2007. From 2007, Japan will then have a self-propelling niche market for residential, grid-connected PV systems. The tentative target price of 5 US$/$W_p$ can be reached in 2001. An important question is what government subsidies are required to reach the docking point and how do these subsidies relate to learning investments provided by the other actors in the energy system. Many of these actors are inside Japan, but success also relies on learning investments continuing outside of Japan. In the following analysis, the experience curve approach is used to discuss learning investments and global learning.

At a system price of 1.1 US$/$W_p$, PV will start to compete with fossil technologies on the utility market for central power stations. This price is therefore the point of reference for calculating the learning investments. Figure 3.11 shows the learning investments for the PV-Roof programme from 1994 to 1998 and forecasts for an unchanged programme which can reach a target price at 3 US$/$W_p$. The diagram also shows the part of the learning investments which is paid by government subsidies. The difference is the share of learning investments paid by the investor. The utility law stipulates that the investor can sell surplus production to the utilities at buy-back rates equal to end-user prices. Ultimately, the investor's learning investments are shared between the investor and the utilities.

The total government subsidy for the programme until 1998 is about 200 million US$. A further 1300 million US$ will be needed to reach the docking point of 3 US$/$W_p$ in 2007. The total subsidy required to create a self-propelling niche market is thus 1.5 billion US$. Figure 3.11 shows, however, that the learning investments stimulated by the PV-Roof programme are much larger than the subsidy. Until 1998, the programme stimulated market actors to provide additional learning investments of about 300 million US$, and will stimulate further learning

## Figure 3.11. Investments and Subsidies in PV-Roof Programme

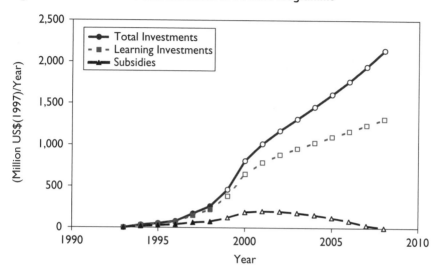

Investments and subsidies in Japan for an unchanged PV-roof programme until 2007. Open points are forecasts.

investments of 6900 million US$ until the docking point. If the programme is continued, the market will have multiplied the government subsidy by a factor of 5.7, to yield total learning investments from government and market actors in Japan of 8.7 billion US$.

If a self-sustaining niche market for PV-systems is reached at 5 US$/W$_p$, public subsidies can be phased out over the next few years. The demand for learning investments remains the same, but the total subsidy required to reach the docking point is reduced to 700 million US$.

The Japanese programme relies on an active world market for PV-modules. Learning for PV-systems is global, and achieving 3.0 US$/Wp requires learning investments in modules and BOS outside of Japan. The US and the EU have announced PV programmes similar to Japan's programme, and the scenario in Figures 3.10 and 3.11 assumes that these programmes will be realised. The experience curve analysis shows, that in order to reach 3 US$/Wp in 2007, market actors outside

## Figure 3.12. Japan's PV-Roof Programme and World PV-Markets

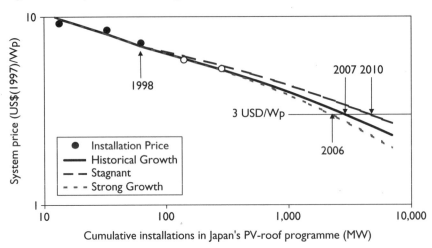

Time for Docking into the Japanese niche market in different scenarios for the world PV-market, assuming an unchanged Japanese programme.

## Figure 3.13. Learning Investments in Residential PV Systems

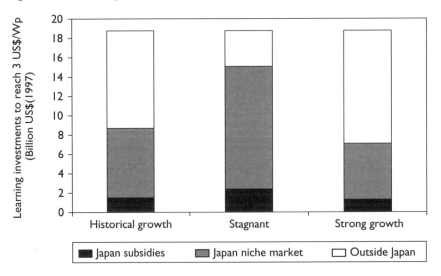

Sharing of Learning Investments in different scenarios for the world PV-market, but assuming an unchanged Japanese programme.

of Japan must invest 10 billion US$ in learning about PV-systems. A stagnant or accelerating market outside of Japan will effect both the target year and the cost of the Japanese programme. This is illustrated in Figures 3.12 and 3.13.

The scenario labelled "Historical Growth" is identical to the case in Figures 3.10 and 3.11. "Stagnant" world market means zero growth for PV systems outside of Japan. In this case, the annual new capacity installed on these markets decreases to 100-150 MW for the period of 2000-2010. The possibilities for the Japanese programme to learn from other programmes are reduced and the time for docking into the niche market slips to 2010. A world market that expands at the rate of 25% per year ("Strong Growth") will boost the Japanese programme and reduce the docking time by 1 to 2 years. Such high growth rates were observed for nuclear power in the 1960s and 1970s.

Figure 3.13 indicates a dramatic redistribution of learning investments among the scenarios. The total learning investments remain the same for the three scenarios, but the Japanese share increases from 45% in "Historical Growth" to 80% in a "Stagnant" world market. If world markets expand, learning investments in Japan will be reduced to about one third of the total learning investments necessary to reach the docking point of 3 US$/$W_p$. Stagnant world markets require 60% more subsidies than in the base case, or 2.4 billion US$ compared with 1.5 billion US$. A stagnant world market for PV will require more domestic resources to dock PV to the niche market for residential, grid-connected systems, but would also be expected to give Japanese industry a "cutting edge" on PV technology.

The calculations for the first decade of 2000 are scenarios, not forecasts. They indicate how experience curves can be used to support policy targets and measures. The model used for the calculations[26] will be refined, as more is understood about niche markets and the learning patterns for components in the PV-system. For instance,

---

26. PV-GOL$^2$D, (GlObal Learning, Local Deployment) is a simulating model for PV niche markets and compound PV-systems (Wene, to be published)

global learning is a tenable assumption for the modules, but BOS may contain components that are country specific and learning for BOS may therefore not be completely global. However, such refinements will not change the substance of the results. Firstly, considerable resources are necessary to dock PV-systems into large niche markets, but the financial involvement from the government can be limited and phased out over time. Secondly, global learning influences the ability to reach national targets. Concerted action among governments and energy market actors is needed in order to create balanced portfolios of energy technologies to manage the risk of climate change.

# CHAPTER 4: DYNAMICS OF LEARNING AND TECHNOLOGY COMPETITION

*This chapter presents two modelling experiments. The models look at the technology learning required to create a low-cost path leading to stabilisation of $CO_2$ emissions during the next century. The experiments demonstrate how experience curves are used to explore technology options and identify areas where government intervention may be necessary to satisfy societal goals.*

## The Effect of Learning on Estimates of $CO_2$ Mitigation Cost

Macroeconomic analysis indicates that substantial costs are required to reduce global $CO_2$ emissions (see e.g., Manne and Richels, 1992; Nordhaus, 1994; IEA, 1998). One of the reasons for the high cost discussed in the Roadmap in Figure 2.3 is that most clean technologies are still too expensive to compete with fossil technologies in present markets. Macroeconomic calculations indicate that implementation of these technologies requires high $CO_2$ taxes or high-price emissions permits, which increase the cost of $CO_2$ reduction. However, if learning investments for $CO_2$ benign technologies can be provided, they may reduce the cost barriers. Including the effects of technology learning in the analysis will thus drastically reduce the estimated costs for $CO_2$ reductions.

A low-cost path to the stabilisation of $CO_2$ emissions in the next century requires sustained and targeted learning investments over the next few decades. The following discussion focuses on the time horizon for the learning investments and on the need to allocate scarce learning opportunities toward promising technologies.

A simple model for the breakaway from the present carbon baseline will illustrate the need for sustained and targeted efforts. The baseline in the model is defined in Figure 4.1, which shows global carbon intensity as a function of cumulative GDP. Information on carbon emissions and world GDP are from World Energy Outlook (IEA, 1998). The global economic system can be considered as one learning system with carbon as one of its inputs, GDP as output, and carbon intensity as a measure of performance. The baseline in Figure 4.1 therefore represents a learning curve for carbon. The progress ratio is 79%, indicating a decarbonisation rate of 21%. These values can be compared to the progress ratio of 82% found for the US economy during the period from 1850 to 1990 (Nakicenovic, 1997; see also footnote in chapter 2, section 2).

**Figure 4.1. Carbon Intensity of World Economy, 1971-2020**

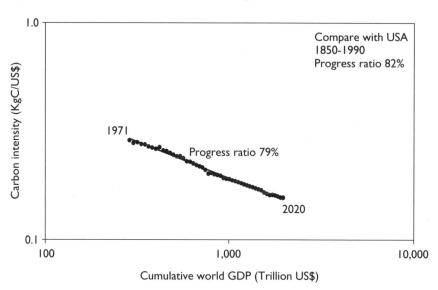

The learning curve for carbon in the world economy calculated from the World Energy Outlook 1998 (IEA, 1998).

**Figure 4.2. Carbon Intensity Paths, 1971-2060**

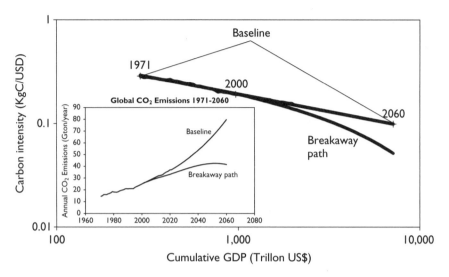

Baseline extended to 2060, and an alternative carbon intensity path leading to a breakaway from the baseline resulting in stabilisation of $CO_2$ emissions around 2050. The in-folded picture shows the annual $CO_2$ emissions corresponding to the baseline and the breakaway path.

The carbon baseline is extended through 2060 in Figure 4.2, assuming the WEO GDP-growth rate for the period 1995 to 2020 remains constant over the period 2021 to 2060. The interior figure shows the corresponding annual $CO_2$ emissions. Staying on the present baseline means that $CO_2$ emissions will quadruple between 1990 and 2060. Figure 4.2 also shows a carbon intensity path that breaks away from the baseline and leads to a stabilisation of emissions around 2050. This path is generated by increasing the progress ratio after 2000, until it in 2060 is around 50%.[27]

The steadily increasing progress ratio is a result of the increasing deployment of new, climate-friendly technologies. These technologies

---

27. Formally, the alternative path in Figure 4.2 is generated by linearly increasing the experience parameter, E, in the experience curve equation as cumulative GDP increases beyond 2000. The effect is the same as fixing a spring to 2000 and letting the force to breakaway from the baseline increase as the spring is stretched. The procedure is described in Wene (1999).

are from the second category in the Roadmap in Figure 2.3, and include photovoltaics and biomass technologies. The difference between the baseline and the breakaway path provides learning opportunities for these technologies, which substitute for alternative fossil technologies otherwise installed in the baseline. The new technologies are usually more expensive than their fossil alternatives, and the breakaway path therefore has additional costs compared with the baseline during the first years. These additional costs are equal to the learning investments for the new technologies. As deployment continues along the breakaway path, the experience effect reduces the cost of the new technologies. As the new technologies break even with their fossil alternatives, the costs for the baseline and for the breakaway path will be the same. As learning continues, the costs for the breakaway path will be less than those for the baseline, because the younger technologies in the breakaway path will learn faster than the older ones in the baseline.

The breakaway model in Figure 4.2 presents an extremely aggregated, top-down view of the world. Its purpose is to explain how the experience effect may modify cost estimates for $CO_2$ reduction and to demonstrate how cost depends on the way new technologies share learning opportunities. The next section introduces an advanced optimising model which verifies these cost trends through a bottom-up construction of baseline and breakaway paths.

For the immediate future, the technologies for the breakaway path are close to market, such as technologies to improve energy efficiency including energy-efficient building envelopes, heat pumps and compact fluorescent light. Gas technologies may also increase their shares faster than in the baseline case. However, to continue increasing the slope of the carbon learning curve requires new supply technologies with no net emissions of $CO_2$ during their operation. For the modelling experiment, the $CO_2$-benign and market-ripe technologies fill 98% of the gap between the baseline and the breakaway path around 2000. Their share of avoided $CO_2$ emissions decreases to less than 50% in 2010, which opens up learning opportunities for new supply technologies such as renewables. For illustration, the effect of deploying photovoltaics is analysed.

Figure 4.3 shows the additional cost for photovoltaics until 2030, if this technology is the only new carbon-free supply technology. The progress ratio for photovoltaics is 79%. All the other technologies used to generate the breakaway path are ready for the market and their additional costs small. The curve in Figure 4.3 therefore estimates the cost for the breakaway path compared with the baseline, albeit under the unrealistic assumption that PV is the only new renewable supply technology.

Within a short time horizon of less than ten years, the photovoltaic alternative appears costly. However, as experience accumulates the price of photovoltaic systems decreases, and in 2013 PV breaks even with alternative fossil technologies in the baseline.[28] As learning

**Figure 4.3. Additional Annual Cost for Photovoltaics**

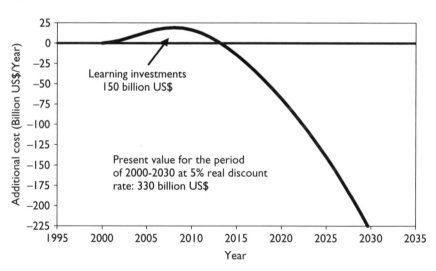

Additional cost for photovoltaics in the breakaway path from 2000 to 2030.

---

28. Fossil technologies also learn, however, at a much lower rate than new renewable technology such as photovoltaics. See the discussion in section 1.1 and Figure 1.5.

continues beyond the break-even point, electricity from PV becomes cheaper than electricity from fossil fuels. Instead of additional costs for a renewable alternative, the longer time horizon identifies these costs as learning investments, which are recovered after 2013. With a 5% real rate of discount, the present value of the PV alternative is positive and some 330 billion US$.[29] The undiscounted sum of learning investments from 2000 to 2013 is 150 billion US$.

The cost curve in Figure 4.3 illustrates how technology learning through market experience overcomes the cost barrier and provides profitable investments. However, the breakaway path cannot be achieved by a single carbon-free technology. Availability of renewable resources, reliability of the energy system and the risk of technology failure require a portfolio of carbon-free technologies. We will use our simple model to explore the properties of a portfolio consisting of three renewable technologies. For illustration, the technologies should represent different learning rates and positions on the experience curve. The technologies are photovoltaics with a progress ratio of 79%, biomass liquefaction with a ratio of 82%, and electricity or heat from biomass with a ratio of 92%.[30]

Figure 4.4 shows the cost curves for the portfolio and for the three technologies in the portfolio. The three technologies share equally between them the learning opportunities used for only one technology in Figure 4.3. This means that photovoltaics have one third of the annual learning investments compared with the earlier case, which delays break-even by five years until 2019. Technologies to produce

---

29. Price reductions proceed beyond break-even, but the calculations recognise a lower cost limit due to resource constraints at 2 Uscents/kWh.

30. The progress ratio for photovoltaics is from the analysis in section 2.4. The analysis of the experience curve for Brasilian ethanol provides an average progress ratio of 80%. 82% is therefore a "conservative" estimate, which is equal to the most probable value for a progress ratio found by Dutton and Thomas (1984). The ATLAS data indicate a progress ratio of 85% for electricity from biomass, but this value is uncertain because the measurement is only made over one doubling of cumulative output. Like wind power, technology to convert biomass into heat or electricity contains many well established technical components and one therefore expects a larger progress ratio than for photovoltaics and biomass liquefaction. A 92% progress ratio represents an educated guess lying between the 85% from ATLAS data and the 96% measured for wind power.

electricity from biomass or heat from biomass start with prices much closer to the commercial alternatives, and therefore reach the break-even point at 2016 in spite of the fact that they have a much smaller learning rate. Automotive fuels from biomass are 3 to 4 times more expensive than their fossil alternatives (IEA/AFIS, 1998), while the price for PV in 2000 is 10 times larger than the fossil alternative. The present experience of PV is, however, less than of biomass liquefaction, and equal learning opportunities have a larger effect on PV prices than on prices for biomass liquefaction. Different starting points therefore explain the different behaviours of PV and biomass liquefaction in the beginning of the period. Progress ratios and assumptions on lower price limits explain the cost curves at the end of the period.[31]

**Figure 4.4. Additional Annual Cost for Technology Portfolio**

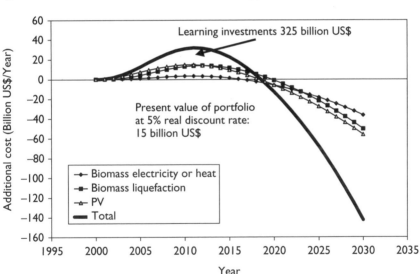

Additional annual costs for a technology portfolio with three technologies which are deployed with equal weights to reduce $CO_2$ emissions.

---

31. Wene (1999) discusses the input data to the Breakaway Model and gives a fuller description of the results.

The portfolio breaks even in 2019 and the sum of portfolio learning investments is 325 billion US$. The portfolio sum is slightly less than the sum of learning investments for the individual technologies, because they break even at different times and there will be some cross-subsidies to the latecomers from early achievers. The present value of the portfolio for the period of 2000-2030 is positive but reduced to 15 billion US$ from the 330 billion US$ for a single technology. The reason for this reduction is that the portfolio has three technologies competing for the same learning opportunities, which delays break-even for all three technologies. Without the learning constraint the value of the portfolio would be higher than for a single technology.

The modelling experiment illustrates that the learning opportunities provided by the market represent a resource which is used to induce technology development. The experiment thus reflects the analysis of R&D and deployment policies in Chapter 2, where the conclusion was that the industrial learning process depends on market deployment of the technology in order to generate substantial price reductions. Comparing the present value between the cases for one and three technologies shows that the scarcity cost for learning opportunities may be considerable. This raises the question of how to allocate this scarce resource among the three technologies. In a real case, the distribution of learning investment among technologies determines this allocation. The simple model treats the allocation as given by the shares of the individual technologies in the $CO_2$ abatement measures. Varying these shares and calculating the corresponding present value of the technology portfolio provides the map in Figure 4.5. The cross indicates the position of the equal shares portfolio in Figure 4.4. The value of the technology portfolio varies between 10 to 200 billion US$, depending on allocation of learning opportunities. Relative to the equal shares portfolio, increasing the weight of photovoltaics or biomass liquefaction improves the return on learning investments.

More detailed studies of energy systems are necessary to find what combinations of technologies are feasible, considering, for instance, available energy resources and distribution of energy demand. A

**Figure 4.5. Present Value of Technology Portfolio**

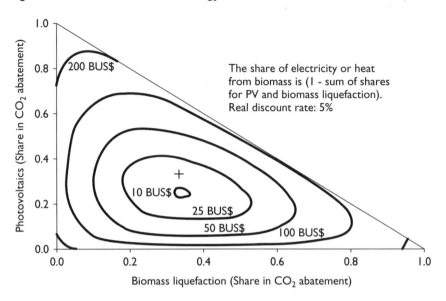

The share of electricity or heat from biomass is (1 - sum of shares for PV and biomass liquefaction). Real discount rate: 5%

Present value for the period from 2000 to 2030 for a portfolio of three technologies. The cross refers to a portfolio where the technologies share equally in $CO_2$ abatement. The present value for such a portfolio is 15 billion US$. The smallest value of the portfolio is 10 billion US$.

realistic portfolio analysis must include several more technologies beside the ones in our simple model, notably, to enable and support other technologies, or to spread technology risk, or to ensure diversification in future energy systems. For instance, the map suggests that the portfolio should have a large share of PV, but this is not possible without storage technologies. Initially promising technologies may not perform or may prove to have properties which exclude deployment. To hedge against such technology risk requires redundancies in the portfolio. However, adding technologies to the portfolio will increase the need for learning investments, and if the added technologies compete for the same learning opportunities, they will delay break-even and reduce the present value of the portfolio. An efficient portfolio must balance allocation of learning opportunities against the need to diversify energy supply and to spread technology risk.

The top-down, breakaway model for global learning and reduction of $CO_2$ emissions suggests three observations regarding $CO_2$ mitigating technologies:

- The experience effect provides a low-cost path for stabilisation of $CO_2$ emissions during the new century.

- The low-cost path requires considerable, sustained and targeted learning investments during the next decades.

- Learning opportunities and learning investments are both scarce resources. A technology portfolio must balance the allocation of learning opportunities against the need to diversify supply and manage technology risk.

## Competition for Learning Investments

The top-down modelling experiments in the previous section indicate that learning periods of one to two decades are needed to reach break-even for renewable technologies with large potential such as photovoltaics and biomass. In the short term, learning investments will appear as an extra cost which is not recoverable. A myopic, least-cost approach will therefore ignore these technologies which are currently expensive but may have a high propensity for learning and for becoming cost-efficient. The case studies in Chapter 3 showed that the policy-maker has several instruments that can be used to overcome the myopic view and to stimulate learning investments.

These case studies only indicate how the policy-maker can intervene into the competition for learning opportunities in an efficient way. Before deciding how to design the intervention, the public policy-maker must consider why he should intervene to ensure learning investments for some technologies but not for others. From the top-down model in the previous section it was seen that learning investments could provide a low-cost path to $CO_2$ stabilisation. The model is unable, however, to recommend which technologies merit support and how learning opportunities in the market should be allocated among these technologies. The allocation of learning opportunities is achieved through learning investments so policy discussions can focus on the need to provide these investments. The policy-maker thus needs technology-specific answers, which explicitly consider the long-range competition for learning investments. Such analysis requires a bottom-up, systems engineering approach.

Many energy systems engineering models are time-stepped, i.e., they consider investments to be taken from a myopic year-by-year perspective. They capture learning in commercial technologies, but cannot analyse the competition for learning investments. Models to describe such competition must be able to look beyond the cost barriers in Figures 4.3 and 4.4 and allocate learning investments to achieve the best performance possible for the complete energy system within a long time horizon.[32] The time horizon must extend at least to 2030. "Best performance" is usually synonymous with "least-cost". The use of experience curves with such models creates considerable mathematical difficulties, because the curves are highly non-linear with increasing return to scale. Results from three different models have been published: Message (Messner, 1997), Genie (Mattsson and Wene, 1997; and Mattsson, 1997) and MARKAL (Seebregts et al., 1998). The Genie results for the global electricity system are discussed here.

Genie considers four world regions with some possibility of natural gas trade among them. Fossil fuel prices rise as resources are depleted. Demands for electricity and for fossil fuels outside the electricity sector are specified externally and are based on scenarios from the U.S. Energy Information Administration (EIA, 1996), the International Atomic Energy Agency (IAEA, 1991) and the joint scenarios from the

---

32. In the technical language of the modelling trade, the requirements are synonymous with "a perfect-foresight, optimising model". The objective for the model is minimum present cost at r% real discount rate. Introducing experience curves for technologies in the model creates non-convex problems, which have several local minima. Finding the global minimum may require several hundred hours of computing time. However important the global minimum may be to the mathematician, the local minima are of large interest to the policy analyst because they represent stable solutions for the model indicating lock-in or lock-out situations in the real world.

International Institute for Applied Systems Analysis and World Energy Conference (IIASA/WEC, 1995). Eleven electric technologies are considered. Beside conventional fossil fuel, hydro and nuclear technologies, the technologies include advanced coal, natural gas combined cycle (NGCC), wind power, fuel cells, photovoltaics (PV), and a hybrid technology consisting of photovoltaics and hydrogen fuel cells (PV-H2). The hybrid technology uses photovoltaics to produce electricity and hydrogen during the solar hours, and the fuel cell to produce electricity from hydrogen during the rest of the day. Mattsson (1997) uses the following progress ratios for the investment costs: photovoltaic systems, 82%, fuel cells and the hybrid PV-H2, 85%, wind and NGCC, 88%, and advanced coal, 95%.[33]

Ignoring the experience effect, the modeller usually finds a single attractive path leading to a stable best or least-cost solution. Experience curves, however, connect future price expectations with current investments so that the cost of a technology becomes dependent on the earlier history of the energy system. The system can therefore create many alternative, low-cost paths by providing or not providing learning investments for specific technologies. Once it has started to develop a specific path, it cannot, however, shift to an alternative path without extra costs. Each path represents attractive configurations of the system because each provides a stable, low-cost solution. The experience curves thus mimic the path-dependence of technology development discussed in evolutionary economics (Cimoli and Dosi, 1995; Kemp, 1997).

The Genie model represents alternative paths through local optima, which are points with local, least-cost solutions for the development of the electricity system. For the policy analyst, these local minima therefore contain the interesting results from the modelling

---

33. Mattsson's (1997) assumptions for investments costs are consistent with information in the sources quoted in this book. Joskow and Rose (1985) finds 95% progress ratio for the investment cost of supercritical coal. EU-ATLAS (Marsh 1998) gives 87% for the total investment cost of wind power plants in the EU, i.e., wind turbines and site preparations, indicating that the learning rate for the site specific investments is much higher than for the wind turbines. The data of Claesson (1999) indicate a progress ratio for NGCC around 90% in a stable market.

## Figure 4.6. Technology Paths for the Global Electricity System

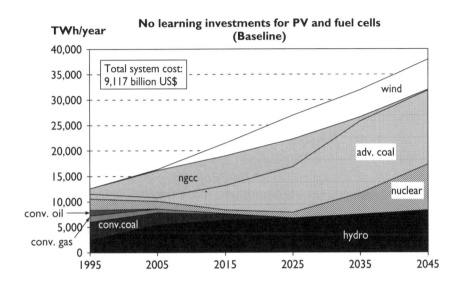

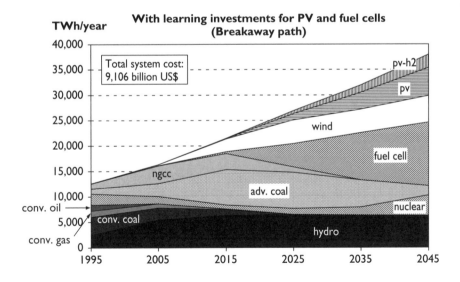

Local optima obtained by the Genie model showing two different but stable development paths for the global electricity system. The paths have the same present costs. The real rate of discount is 5%. (Mattsson, 1997).

experiment, because they simulate stable situations with lock-in or lockout of technologies.

Figure 4.6 shows two different but stable development paths for the global electricity system. The two paths emerge from the same set of assumptions on technology properties, fossil fuel resources and demands. The difference between the two paths is the allocation of learning opportunities. In the first case, photovoltaics and fuel cells do not receive any learning investments, while in the second case there is large deployment of these technologies over the next decades, leading to break even for them around 2025. An interesting result is that the present costs of the two paths are almost identical. This is consistent with the results from the top-down model in the previous section.

The two paths in Figure 4.6 represent baseline development and a breakaway alternative. These two paths are represented in Figure 4.7. In the baseline, the emissions from the global electricity system increase by a factor of two between 1995 and 2045, while on the breakaway path emissions in 2045 are at the same level as in 1995. The interior diagram displays emissions as carbon learning curves for the global electricity system, and indicates that the path with no learning investments for PV and fuel cells, on average, follows the WEO baseline with a 79% progress ratio (compare with Figure 4.1). The variation around the baseline has a very interesting interpretation in terms of lock-in to existing fossil fuel technologies.

During the first two decades, the technologies in the baseline use more natural gas but less coal than the technologies in the breakaway path. The effect is visible both in the annual emissions curve and in the learning curve representation. Until 2015, emissions from the electricity system are smaller in the baseline than in the breakaway path. A myopic look at the carbon learning curve in 2000 would actually indicate a progress ratio of 44%, suggesting that the present growth of natural gas combined cycle plants would provide more than the necessary $CO_2$ reductions for the electricity system. However, by 2010 the system depletes its inexpensive natural gas supplies and turns to advanced coal. In spite of increasing shares for wind power,

## Figure 4.7. Emissions of Carbon Dioxide from Global Electricity System

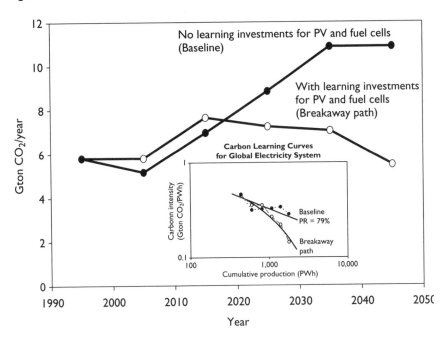

Annual emissions of carbon dioxide from the two paths for the global electricity system shown in Figure 4.8. The in-fold is a learning curve representation of the emissions. The full drawn lines in the in-fold show the carbon learning curves corresponding to the WEO baseline and a breakaway path as discussed in the previous section.

the carbon intensity in the Genie baseline actually increases between 2015 and 2035, until in 2045 when investments in nuclear power bring the intensity back to the WEO baseline. NGCC, advanced coal and wind power receive all of the learning investments, and the Genie baseline effectively locks in to fossil fuels with wind power as the only renewable technology.

The breakaway path still provides markets and learning investments for NGCC and advanced coal, but only as intermediary technologies awaiting maturity for photovoltaics, fuel cells and hybrid PV-H2. The annual growth rate for PV and fuel cells during the first decades of the next century is 30%, which is similar to what has been observed for NGCC and nuclear power. The growth rate levels off to less than 10% per year after 2025.

The breakaway path has a higher annual cost than the baseline until 2025. As learning continues for PV and fuel cells, these additional costs are eventually recovered. Advanced coal and wind power may still require some learning investments in the baseline the amounts, however, are small compared with what is needed for PV, fuel cells and PV-H2 in the breakaway path. The difference in annual costs in Figure 4.8 measures the need for learning investments to achieve the breakaway path. Learning investments from 1995 to 2025 amount to 400 billion US$.

Figure 4.8 shows why policy interventions may be necessary. Learning investments will be needed over a period of 15 to 20 years, which is a long investment horizon from the market point of view. There is therefore considerable risk that the electric energy system will follow the baseline

**Figure 4.8. Cost Difference between Breakaway Path and Baseline**

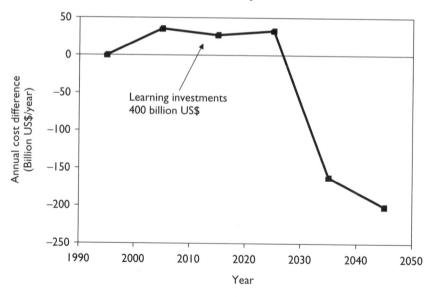

The cost difference between the breakaway path and the baseline from 1995 to 2025 is equal to the learning investments required for the breakaway path.

without policy intervention. The baseline leads to unacceptably high levels of $CO_2$ emissions. The policy-maker therefore needs to identify a portfolio of technologies to breakaway from the baseline and to ensure that the technologies in the portfolio receive learning investments.

From the modelling experiment with Genie the following conclusions can be drawn:

■ The experiment verifies the observation that the experience effect can provide a low-cost path to stabilisation of $CO_2$ emissions from the energy system, but to realise this path requires considerable learning investments over the next decades.

■ The competition for learning investment can result in a lock-in to baseline technologies and lockout of technologies which would be required to breakaway from the baseline. The risk of lockout provides a rationale for policy measures to ensure learning investments for the breakaway technologies.

## Uncertainty about Learning

The policy-maker must consider risks connected to technology portfolios. Here, the risks due to uncertainties in the experience curve analysis are of interest. The experience effect links technology development directly to technology investments in the energy system. In the experience curve analysis, events at two different levels thus cause uncertainties about improvements in technology performance.

■ *Uncertainty about deployment and global learning.* This uncertainty on the system level reflects the ability to provide learning opportunities for the portfolio technologies. Will the technology be deployed in the energy system? Will deployment also lead to efficient global learning?

■ *Uncertainty about ability to learn.* This uncertainty on the technology level reflects the future ability of a technology to continue learning. What is the progress ratio for a new technology? Will the learning rate remain constant for technologies, which already have proven their ability to learn on the market but not yet reached break even?

Some of the uncertainty about deployment and global learning can be resolved through government policies and concerted action between governments. Further studies of experience curves and technology learning will elicit the relationship between local deployment and global learning. However, balancing local deployment and global learning is a complex process, and the future outcome of this balance will always remain a source of uncertainty for the policy analyst. Methodologically, the analyst will be able to estimate the effect of this uncertainty by scenario analysis.

The second uncertainty refers to the value of progress ratios and the shape of experience curves, and represents a specific form of technology risk. For instance, the experience curve for photovoltaics must be extrapolated over several orders of magnitude before it reaches cost levels comparable to conventional, fossil fuel technologies. Small changes in progress ratios will change learning investments considerably and thus the conditions for long-range competitiveness. There may also be cases where the lack of deployment hinders measurement of the progress ratio, and initial estimates must be based on comparisons with similar technologies. We have also seen knees in the experience curve. When these knees are due to changes in the business environment as discussed in section 2.4, they represent only short-term readjustments of the price-cost relationships. Technological structural change speeds up the learning and is a beneficial surprise for the policy-maker. However, there may also be knees due to other factors in the learning system, e.g., reaching a physical limit to improvements for a part of the system. Such limits may be unknown when the decision is taken and represent a real technological risk.

Uncertainty about the ability to learn can only be resolved by deployment, i.e. by making the learning investments. In this situation experience curve analysis can provide valuable support for the decision-maker, by looking at the consequences of uncertainties and by suggesting robust decisions on deployment.

### Figure 4.9. Photovoltaics: Year of 50 GW Cumulative Capacity

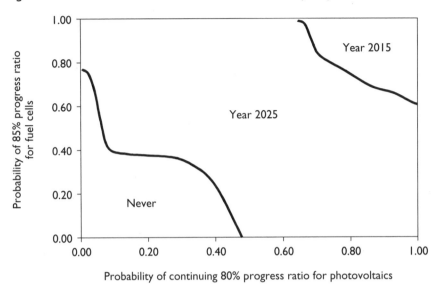

Deployment of photovoltaics to obtain a least-cost energy system. Results from a stochastic version of the Genie model (Mattsson, 1998).

The model discussed in section 4.2 has been used to investigate the effects of a knee in the experience curve for photovoltaics and of a too optimistic initial estimate of the progress ratio for fuel cells. The uncertainty about PV is whether it will continue to show a progress ratio of 80%, or whether it will level off to 90% after having achieved a certain amount of experience (set to 5 GW cumulative production in the model). There is little information about fuel cells, but progress ratios of 85% and 92% are a reasonable range for the experience curve. The uncertainty is assumed to be resolved at cumulative productions of 50 GW, respectively. The uncertainty may resolve over time, but only if learning investments up to 50 GW really are made!

Diagram 4.9 shows the year when the uncertainty is resolved as a function of the probability for a continuous 80% progress ratio for PV and a 85% progress ratio for fuel cells. Resolving the uncertainty in 2015 means that the model favours maximum rates of deployment in spite of the uncertainty, while "never" indicates that the technology should not receive any learning investments. In the latter case, uncertainty about the learning rates excludes the technology from the cost-efficient solution. We conclude that learning investments in PV should be stimulated, if the decision-maker believes that there is a 50% probability that PV will continue to have an 80% progress ratio. At a lower probability, the conclusion depends on the probability for a high learning rate for fuel cells. The reason for this coupling between PV and fuel cells is the hybrid PV-fuel cell technology, which utilises the learning investments from both technologies

## Managing the Balance between Global Learning and Local Deployment

The experience effect provides a mechanism for technology-controlled, low-cost stabilisation of $CO_2$ emissions. The analysis suggests a proactive, globally oriented strategy based on portfolios of generic technologies. As each new technology will need learning investments, there is a need to keep the number of portfolio technologies small in order to reduce total learning investments and bring a portfolio to maturity within the foreseeable future. Efficient global learning requires local deployments which are coherent on a global scale.

It is important to realise the limitations of the global analysis and the dangers inherent in interventions to try to force global learning. Efficient and robust energy systems need local flexibility, diversification of supply and the ability to manage technology risk. Flexibility requires decisions on deployment to consider local resources and demands. To manage risk, spreading investments over many technologies can ensure local variety and reduce the risk that failure of one technology leads to major failures in all systems. The management of flexibility and technology risk thus requires local autonomy for decisions on deployment, which is in conflict with the concerted action necessary to achieve maximum effect from learning investments.

A balance between coherent global learning and autonomous local deployment is established through the collective action of the actors on local, national and international energy markets. Strong actors are multinational and national energy companies, financial institutions and governments. Analysis in the previous two sections raises the question as to whether new institutions are needed to move the point of balance towards increased coherency in order to have cost-efficient $CO_2$ mitigation technologies available in the next century. Some institutions may already have increased this coherency, e.g., Joint Implementation and the Clean Deployment Mechanism. A purposeful change of the balance will, however, require much more concerted action.

# CHAPTER 5: CONCLUSIONS – IMPLICATIONS FOR ENERGY TECHNOLOGY POLICY

*"Would you tell me, please, which way I ought to go from here?"*
*"That depends a good deal on where you want to get to",*
*said the Cat.*
*"I don't much care where—" said Alice.*
*"Then it doesn't matter which way you go," said the Cat.*
*"– so long as I get* somewhere," *Alice added as an explanation.*
*"Oh, you're sure to do that," said the Cat, "if only you walk long enough."*
*Lewis Carroll, Alice's Adventures in Wonderland*

Conclusions emerge for three areas relevant to energy technology: policy making in the form of strategic decisions on energy technology policy, design and monitoring of policy measures and development of tools to aid analysis and monitoring.

A general message to policy makers comes from the basic philosophy of the experience curve. Learning requires continuous action, and future opportunities are therefore strongly coupled to present activities. If we want cost-efficient, $CO_2$-mitigation technologies available during the first decades of the new century, these technologies must be given the opportunity to learn in the current marketplace. Deferring decisions on deployment will risk lock-out of these technologies, i.e., lack of opportunities to learn will foreclose these options making them unavailable to the energy system. From this point of view, the present success of the increasingly efficient combined-cycle technology may significantly reduce $CO_2$ emissions from the electricity sector until 2010, but may prove fatal for new non-fossil electric technology after

2010. Focusing policy measures in the period of 2008-2012 may severely restrict options beyond 2012.

The encouraging result from the modelling experiments here is that portfolios of new technologies can drastically reduce the total cost for the transition to a low-carbon economy by the middle of the new century. However, the low-cost path to $CO_2$-stabilisation requires large investments in technology learning over the next decades. The learning investments are provided through market deployment of technologies not yet commercial, in order to reduce the cost of these technologies and make them competitive with conventional fossil-fuel technologies. Governments can use several policy instruments to ensure that market actors make the large-scale learning investments in environment-friendly technologies. Measures to encourage niche markets for new technologies are one of the most efficient ways for governments to provide learning opportunities. The learning investments are recovered as the new technologies mature, illustrating the long-range financing component of cost-efficient policies to reduce $CO_2$ emissions. The time horizon for learning stretches over several decades, which require long-term, stable policies for energy technology.

Efficient strategies to make $CO_2$-friendly technologies available in the early decades of the new century must rely on international co-operation. Technology learning needs to be global, but technology deployment will be local. This calls for a long-term, collective effort, requiring local actions which lead to joint, coherent learning on a global scale. On the other hand, local autonomy is needed in order to ensure efficient use of local resources, meet local demands and spread the risk of technology failures. Therefore, management of the low-cost path to $CO_2$ stabilisation needs institutions and processes to work out a balance between global coherence and local autonomy. In such a balance, a multitude of technology portfolios on different levels can work together to provide opportunities for promising technologies to "ride down the experience curve", while each portfolio retains the variety that ensures the secure and efficient working of local and national markets.

Managing the risks of lock-out, creating niche markets to ensure learning investments and participating in the working out of a balance between coherence and autonomy are issues for strategic decisions to bring in $CO_2$ mitigation technologies. The case studies show that experience curves can also support the design and monitoring of policy measures.

The case of solar heating shows how experience curves can be used to set cost targets that can be reached through targeted RD&D support and to provide a defensible rationale for terminating public support when the technology has reached maturity or does not show any learning. In this case, reaching the point where commercial interests can take over calls for only limited investments in learning. When larger investments are needed and when market actors must supply the major share of such investments, a package of policy measures is needed to bring technologies to the point where they are commercially viable. Besides targeted RD&D support, such packages will contain measures to encourage large-scale deployment on the market. There are several such measures available to the policy maker, from direct subsidies and tax exemptions to mandated grid prices and regulatory instruments. The wind energy case suggests a way for using experience curves to assess the efficiency of policy packages for deployment.

An efficient policy package should support the creation or exploitation of niche markets, where the specific properties of the technology are given a price premium. Experience curves are tools for designing entry and exit strategies for public policy interventions on such markets. The Japanese photovoltaic systems programme demonstrates how interventions are used to set up the niche markets, but also how experience curves are used not only to provide a definite target for the intervention, but also to design an exit strategy for the direct subsidies.

There are only a few explicit examples of the use of experience curves for energy technology policy analysis. Only a few measurements of experience curves for energy technologies are reported in the literature, and these measurements are concentrated in a few technologies. The lack of information and activity is surprising, both in view of the wealth of data and the use of experience curves in other technology areas and in view of the potential benefits to public policy making. One reason for the inactivity in the public area may be that data are proprietary and that information about experience curves has competitive value in designing business strategies. However, information on experience curves is available in other highly competitive markets, and general data on technologies supported by public funds should be available to the policy analyst. This book therefore ends with a call to the developer of analytic tools to engage in making experience curves available to the analyst of energy technology policy. A better quantitative understanding of the factors that drive the experience curve is also needed, as well as of the relationship between national and global learning and the effects from learning in other technology fields. Statistics on market prices and deployment of energy technologies, gathered and disseminated in the same manner as for fuel and energy use, would be of great assistance to the researcher.

# REFERENCES

Abell, D.F. and Hammond, J.S. (1979), "Cost Dynamics: Scale and Experience Effects", in: *Strategic Planning: Problems and Analytical Approaches*, Prentice Hall, Englewood Cliffs, N.J.

Argote, L. and Epple, D. (1990), "Learning Curves in Manufacturing", *Science*, Vol. 247, p. 920.

Arrow, K. (1962), "The Economic Implications of Learning by Doing", *Review of Economic Studies*, p. 155.

Arthur, B. (1990), "Competing technologies: an Overview", in Dosi et al. (Eds), *Technical Change and Economic Theory*, Pinter, London.

Ashby, W. R. (1964), *An Introduction to Cybernetics*, Chapman and Hall and University Paperbacks, London.

Ayres, R.U. and Martinas, K. (1992), "Experience and life cycle: Some analytical implications", *Technovation*, Vol. 12, p. 465.

Boston Consulting Group (1968), *Perspectives on experience*, Boston Consulting Group Inc.

Bundesanzeiger (1994), "Richtlinie zur Förderung der Erprobung von Windenergieanlagen '250 MW Wind' im Rahmen des dritten Programms Energieforschung und Energietechnologien", p. 921, Jahrgang 46, No 24, 4. Februar 1994.

Carlman, I. (1990), "Blåsningen. Svensk vindkraft 1973 till 1990 (Gone with the wind. Wind Power in Sweden 1973 until 1990)", *Geografiska Regionstudier 23*, Uppsala. ISBN 91-506-0824-X. Swedish text with a summary in English.

Cimoli, M. and Dosi, G. (1995), "Technological paradigms, patterns of learning and development: an introductory roadmap", *Journal of Evolutionary Economics*, Vol 5, p. 243.

Claeson, U. (1999), "Using the experience curve to analyze the cost development of the combined cycle gas turbine", *Proceedings IEA Workshop on Experience Curves for Policy Making – The Case of Energy Technologies*, 10-11 May 1999, Stuttgart, Germany, forthcoming.

Cowan, R. (1999), "Learning Curves and Technology Policy: On Technology Competition, Lock-in and Entrenchment", *Proceedings IEA Workshop on Experience Curves for Policy Making – The Case of Energy Technologies*, 10-11 May 1999, Stuttgart, Germany, forthcoming.

Durstewitz, M. (1999), private communication (M. Durstewitz, ISET, Köningstor 59, D-34119 Kassel, Germany)

Durstewitz, M. and Hoppe-Kilpper, M. (1999), "Using information of Germany's '250 MW Wind'-Programme for the Construction of Wind Power experience Curves", *Proceedings IEA Workshop on Experience Curves for Policy Making – The Case of Energy Technologies*, 10-11 May 1999, Stuttgart, Germany, forthcoming.

Dutton, J.M. and Thomas, A. (1984), "Treating Progress Functions as a Managerial Opportunity", *Academy of Management Review*, Vol. 9, p. 235.

EIA (1996), *Annual Energy Outlook 1996*, Energy Information Administration, U.S. Department of Energy, Washington D.C., USA.

Gipe, P. (1995), *Wind Energy comes of age*, John Wiley, N.Y.

Goldemberg, J. (1996), "The evolution of ethanol cost in Brazil", *Energy Policy*, Vol. 24, p. 1127.

Hall, G. and Howell, S. (1985), "The Experience Curve from the Economist's Perspective", *Strategic Management Journal*, Vol. 6, p. 197.

IAEA (1991), "Energy and Electricity Supply and Demand", Key Issues Paper No. 1, *Senior Expert Symposium on Electricity and the Environment*, Helsinki, Finland, 13-17 May 1991.

IEA (1998), *World Energy Outlook*, International Energy Agency/ Organisation for Economic Co-operation and Development, Paris.

IEA/AFIS (1998), *Automotive Fuels Survey, 3: Comparison and Selection*, IEA Implementing Agreement on Advanced Motor Fuels, Automotive fuels information service (IEA/AFIS).

IIASA/WEC (1995), *World Energy Perspectives to 2050 and Beyond*, International Institute for Applied Systems Analysis/World Energy Council, Laxenburg, Austria and London, U.K.

Ikki, O., Tomori, K. and Ohigashi, T. (1999), "The Current Status of Photovoltaic Dissemination Programme in Japan", Resources Total Systems (e-mail: ged02723@nifty.ne.jp), November 1999, Tokyo.

ISET (1999), *Wissenschaftliches Mess- und Evaluierungsprogramm (WMEP) zum Breitentest "250 MW Wind" Jahresauswertung 1998*, Institut für Solare Energieversorgungstechnik, ISET e.V., Köningstor 59, D-34119 Kassel.

Jaskow, P.L. and Rose, N.L. (1985), "The effects of technological change, experience, and environmental regulation on the construction cost of coal-burning generating units", *Rand Journal of Economics*, Vol. 16, p. 1.

Kemp, R. (1997), *Environmental Policy and Technical Change*, Cheltenham, Edward Elgar.

Kleinkauf, W., Durstewitz, M. and Hoppe-Kilpper, M. (1997), "Allgemeine Entwicklung der Kosten der Windstromerzeugung in Deutschland", Institut für Solare Energieversorgungstechnik (ISET), Projektbereich Windenergie, Köningstor 59, D-34119 Kassel, March 1997.

Kline, D. (1998), private communication (D. Kline, NREL, Center for Energy Analysis and Applications, 1617 Cole Blvd, Golden, CO 80401-3393, USA).

Lawitzka, H. (1992), "Lernkurven von sogenannten Technologiefamilien als Strategieinstrument von Forschung und Entwicklung",

*Statusbericht: Selektive Schichten in der Solartechnik*, p. 3, BMFT-Statusseminar, 18.-19. März 1992, Physik-Zentrum Bad Honnef, Germany.

Lawitzka, H. (1999), "Use of Experience Curves within Germany's R&D Programme", *Proceedings IEA Workshop on Experience Curves for Policy Making – The Case of Energy Technologies*, 10-11 May 1999, Stuttgart, Germany, forthcoming.

Manne, A. and Richels, R. (1992), *Buying Greenhouse Insurance: Economic Cost of $CO_2$ Emission Limits*, MIT Press, Cambridge, MA, USA.

Marsh, G. (1998), "Energy Technology Cost Trends: The case of Renewable Energy", Energy Technology Support Unit, Harwell, UK

Mattsson, N. (1997), *Internalizing technological development in energy system models*, Thesis for the Degree of Licentiate of Engineering, Energy Systems Technology, Chalmers University of Technology, Göteborg, Sweden

Mattsson, N. (1999), "Uncertain learning and implications for energy technology policy", *Proceedings IEA Workshop on Experience Curves for Policy Making – The Case of Energy Technologies*, 10-11 May 1999, Stuttgart, Germany, forthcoming.

Mattsson, N. and Wene, C.-O. (1997), "Assessing New Energy Technologies Using an Energy System Model with Endogenized Experience Curves", *Int. Journal of Energy Research*, Vol. 21, p. 385.

Messner, S. (1997), "Endogenized technological learning in an energy systems model", *Journal of Evolutionary Economics*, Vol. 7, p. 291.

Nakicenovic, N. (1996), "Technological Change and Learning", in N. Nakicenovic et al. (eds.), *Climate Change : Integrating Science, Economics and Policy*, CP-96-1, IIASA, Laxenburg, Austria.

Neij, L. (1999), "Cost dynamics of wind power", *Energy*, Vol 24, p. 375

Nitsch, J. (1998), "Probleme der Langfristkostenschätzung – Beispiel Regenerative Energien", Vortrag beim Workshop "Energiesparen – Klimaschutz der sich rechnet", Rotenburg an der Fulda, 8-9 October, 1998.

Nordhaus, W. (1994), *Managing the Global Commons: the Economics of the Greenhouse Effect*, MIT Press, Cambridge, MA, USA.

Seebregts, A.J., Kram, T., Schaeffer, G.J., and Stoffer, A. (1998), "Endogenous Technological Learning: Experiments with MARKAL (Contribution to task 2.3 in the EU-TEEM Project)", *ECN-C–98-064*, Netherlands Energy Research Foundation, Petten, The Netherlands.

Smith, K. (1996), "Systems Approaches to Innovation: Some Policy Issues", in C. Edquist and F. Texier (Eds), *Innovation Systems and European Integration*, Research project within the Targeted Socio-Economic Research Programme of the European Commission (DGXII), CD-ROM, ISBN 91-8219-266-6, Linköping University, Sweden.

Stump, N. (1997), "The 250 MW Wind Programme in Germany – Review and Results", BEO, Forschungszentrum Jülich, Germany

Tsuchiya, H. (1989), "PhotovoltaicCost Based on the Learning Curve", *Proc. Intl. Solar Energy Society Clean & Safe Energy Forever Symposium*, Kobe City, Sep. 4-8, 1989, p.402.

Utility Photovoltaic Group (1994), "Photovoltaics: On the Verge of Commercialization – Summary report", Utility PhotoVoltaic Group, 1800 M Street, NW, Suite 300, Washington, DC 20036-5802, June 1994.

Watanabe, C. (1995), "Identification of the Role of Renewable Energy – A View from Japan's Challenge: The New Sunshine Program", *Renewable Energy*, Vol. 6, p. 237.

Watanabe, C. (1999), "Industrial Dynamism and the Creation of a 'Virtuous Cycle' between R&D, Market Growth and Price Reduction – The Case of Photovoltaic Power Generation (PV) Development in

Japan", *Proceedings IEA Workshop on Experience Curves for Policy Making — The Case of Energy Technologies*, 10-11 May 1999, Stuttgart, Germany, forthcoming.

Wene, C.-O. (1999), "Decarbonisation beyond World Energy Outlook", *Report 1999:1*, ISRN CTH-EST-R – 99:1-SE, Energy Systems Technology Division, Chalmers University of Technology, Gothenburg, Sweden.

Williams, R.H. and Terzian, G. (1993), "A benefit/cost analysis of accelerated development of photovoltaic technology", PU/CEES Report No. 281, Princeton University, N.J., USA.

Windheim, R. (1999), private communication (R. Windheim, BEO, KFA-Jülich, D-52425 Jülich, Germany)

Wright, T.P. (1936), "Factors Affecting the Cost of Airplanes", *Journal of the Aeronautical Sciences*, Vol. 3, p. 122.

# APPENDIX A

## GRAPHIC REPRESENTATION
## OF EXPERIENCE CURVES

# Graphic Representation of Experience Curves

Figures A.1 and A.2 show two different graphic representations of the same experience curve for PV modules (also shown in Figure 1.1).

Figure A.1 is a linear representation. The scales for "Cumulative PV Sales" and "PV Module Price" are linear, which means, that any distances along the axes are directly proportional to the absolute change in cumulative sales and price. The eye sees a very steep initial change in price, but as experience accumulates, the price curve flattens out and progressively more and more cumulative sales are necessary to produce a visible reduction in prices. Comparing with other competitive efforts, one could say that what starts on a downhill track ends up as a long-distance cross-country skiing race, requiring considerable stamina from the competitors. The linear representation explains why some authors maintain that learning or experience effects only appear during the introductory phase of a new product or process. This representation thus emphasises the large initial improvements in performance, but there is a risk that it obscures the continuous, but less dramatic developments in the following phases.

Figure A.2 is a double-logarithmic representation of the same price-cumulative sales relationship as in Figure A.1. The scales for "Cumulative PV Sales" and "PV Module Prices" are logarithmic, which means that any distance along the axes are directly proportional to the relative or percentage change in cumulative sales and price. The experience curve appears as a straight line in this representation. The logarithmic representation emphasises the steady and continuous improvements in performance, but underlines that these improvements always should be seen relative to previous achievements.

The series of right-angle triangles tracing the experience curve illustrate the difference between the two representations. The corners of the triangles are at identical points in the two diagrams, but the triangles themselves appear quite different in the two representations. The base of each triangle corresponds to a doubling of cumulative sales. The first

Figure A.1. Experience Curve for Photovoltaic Modules, 1976-1992

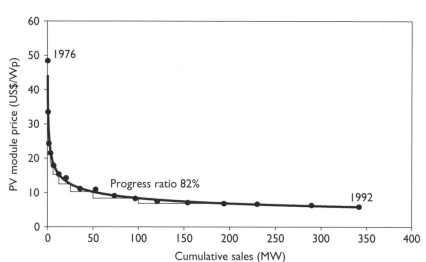

Linear representation of an experience curve.

Figure A.2. Experience Curve for Photovoltaic Modules, 1976-1992

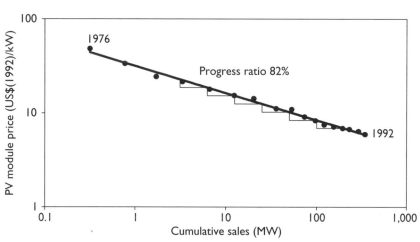

Double-logarithmic representation of an experience curve (same as in Figure A.1).

triangle starts at cumulative sales of 3.125 MW, and thus has a base of 3.125 MW ending at cumulative sales of 6.25 MW (= 2 × 3.125). The bases of the following triangles are 6.25, 12.5, 25, 50 and 100 MW, respectively. The progress ratio of the experience curve is 82%, and thus the height of each triangle corresponds to a price reduction of 18% (= 100-82).

In the logarithmic representation, all triangles have the same shape and size, i.e., they are congruent, mathematically speaking. The identical size and shape of the triangles reflect the fundamental property of the unbroken experience curve, namely that a doubling of cumulative production or sales always produces the same percentage reduction in price. The linear representation, however, reflects absolute changes. The base of each triangle is therefore twice as long as the base of the previous triangle. The height of the triangle becomes smaller as price decreases, and the absolute value of an 18% reduction in price becomes smaller. For instance, the price at 3.125 MW is 22.8 USD/W and the height of the first triangle corresponds to a price reduction of 4.1 USD/kW (= 0.18 × 22.8), but the price at 100 MW is only 8.4 USD/W and the height of the last triangle is therefore only 1.5 USD/W (= 0.18 × 8.4).

The logarithmic representation is used throughout this book. There are two reasons for this choice. The first one is technical and pragmatic. In the logarithmic representation, the basic experience curves appear as straight lines. Straight lines facilitate comparisons between technologies and make it easier to define intercepts, assess goodness of fits to empirical data and deviations from previous trends. It is also possible to follow the experience effect through any orders of magnitude. The second reason is of a more philosophical nature. The logarithmic representation emphasises the long-range, progressive improvements in performance over the initial, more spectacular and obvious ones. This representation thus demonstrates both the needs and the rewards of long-range, sustainable efforts to make new technologies competitive in the marketplace.

# APPENDIX B

## RECOMMENDATIONS FROM IEA WORKSHOP ON EXPERIENCE CURVES FOR POLICY MAKING — THE CASE OF ENERGY TECHNOLOGIES

Stuttgart, May 10-11 1999

# Recommendations from IEA Workshop on Experience Curves for Policy Making – The Case of Energy Technologies, Stuttgart, May 10-11 1999

We are scientists and analysts, who are working in academia, industry and government agencies within IEA countries, and have been assembled in Stuttgart, Germany for two days to discuss the use of experience and learning curves for industrial strategic analysis and for informing and strengthening government energy technology policy. Our agenda has covered many aspects of experience and learning curves: theory and methodology, measurement and analysis, technology forecasting and energy modelling, application to strategy and decision making.

Based on our own experience and on what we have learned during the workshop, we like to make the following observations and recommendations.

- Experience and learning curves are widespread tools for production and strategic analysis within all levels of technology intensive industries. However, they are under-exploited for public policy analysis.

- Experience curves provides the policy analyst with a tool to explore technology and policy options to support the transformation of energy systems and markets towards sustainable development. Specifically, such exploration allows the identification of areas where policy intervention may be necessary to reach goals for environment and climate policies, supports the selection of realistic policy targets and guides the design of policies to reach the targets.

- Experience curves help to clarify the potential benefits of deployment programmes and market transformation programmes. Such programmes allow a technology to learn through the market and create virtuous cycles, which stimulate industry R&D and lead to progressively reduced costs so that the technology can compete with conventional fossil fuel technologies. Costs for deploying not-yet commercial technologies can therefore be considered as "learning investments", which are recovered as the technologies become cost-efficient on the market.

■ Experience curves can help to identify low-cost paths to reach $CO_2$ stabilisation by the middle of the next century. However, realising a low-cost path requires two conditions to be fulfilled: large amounts of learning investments in climate-friendly technologies must be made during the next decades and international collaboration on technology deployment policies is needed to ensure efficient global learning and technology spill-over.

■ The acceleration of experience effects through government policies may provide significant benefits. Issues of government action require further studies. One important issue refers to the risk of lockout of climate-friendly technologies because of lack of learning investments. Governments can intervene to provide or encourage learning investments, but such action has to be balanced against the risk of governments "picking winners" on a level where they do not have the necessary competence. Balancing the two risks cannot be done without reference to broader policy areas of industrial and economic development.

■ Experience curves for energy technology policy require further development to realise their full potential. An urgent issue is the need for quality-controlled and publicly available empirical information on experience curves for new environment friendly technologies. Other important issues that need to be dealt with are

- uncertainty
- inadequacy of relevant data for e. g. costs
- use of analogies and comparison of cases

Putting experience curves in the policy analyst's toolbox requires considerable efforts to establish a database of experience curves for energy technology and development of related methods.

We recommend:

- that experience curves are used to analyse the cost and benefits of programmes to promote environment friendly technologies and the resulting analysis be provided to governments for possible use in deployment policies as part of their support for the research and development.

- that the experience effect is explicitly considered in exploring scenarios to reduce $CO_2$ emissions and calculating the cost of reaching emissions targets

- that the International Energy Agency takes the initiative to an international collaboration on experience curves for energy technology policy analysis

- that this international collaboration is charged with the tasks to disseminate and develop experience curve methodologies for our two first recommendations but also to study the effects of technology spill-over and the needs for concerted action among governments to support global learning.

# APPENDIX C

INTERNATIONAL COLLABORATION ON EXPERIENCE
CURVES FOR ENERGY TECHNOLOGY POLICY
(EXCETP, PRONOUNCED "EXET")

Creating Database, Methodology and Case Studies
to Support Policymaking for Energy Technology

# International Collaboration on Experience Curves for Energy Technology Policy (EXCETP, pronounced "exet")
## Creating database, methodology and case studies to support policymaking for energy technology

## *Aims*

The International Collaboration on Experience Curves for Energy Technology Policy (EXCETP) will provide experience curve data base and methodologies, which together with insights from case studies will support policymaking for energy technology in Participating Countries. It will also aid IEA's Committee on Energy Research and Technology (CERT) in formulating strategies for co-operation on energy research and technology policy. Specifically, EXCETP aims to

1. Analyse *Global Learning and Local Deployment* of technologies with large potentials in many countries, such as photovoltaics, biomass, fuel cells, wind power, advanced power plants, heat pumps, compact fluorescent lamps, high-temperature superconductors as well as technology systems to achieve, e.g., energy efficient lighting, buildings or transport.

2. Disseminate and support the *use of experience curve data and methodology* for policy analysis and decision-making in Participating Countries.

3. Use analysis based on experience curves to support IEA/CERT formulation of strategies for co-operation on energy RD&D and technology policy, recognising the necessity of local autonomy but also *the growing need for coherence of action* on a global scale to manage $CO_2$ emissions.

4. Establish a *quality-controlled database* on empirical information for experience curves.

5. Develop *guidelines* for the construction of experience curves.

6. Support further *development of experience curve methodologies* based on all form of quantitative analysis to explicate and verify experience effects of energy technology implementation.

## *Background*

Experience curves are widespread tools for production and strategic analysis within all levels of technology-intense industry. The fact that gathering experience through acting on competitive markets makes individuals, enterprises and industries do better is at the heart of the experience curve phenomenon. The curves show a simple, quantitative relationship between price and the cumulative production or use of a technology. There is overwhelming support for this price-experience relationship from all fields of industrial activity. It is of great interest to see how experience curves can contribute to the design of energy technology policies. The purpose of this Collaboration is therefore to gather data on experience curves for energy technologies, and through case studies develop methodologies, which can be used to strengthen energy technology policy analysis and decision-making.

The need to consider the experience effect is observed in a document from the IEA Committee on Energy Research and Technology (IEA/CERT) directed to the Energy Ministers at their meeting in Paris for the IEA 25$^{th}$ Anniversary in May 1999. The two-page summary entitled "The Technology Response to Climate Change – A Call for Action" states: "Technology deployment policies can help overcome price barriers since they encourage 'technology learning'. These 'learning investments' will be repaid with more competitive low carbon technologies and new cost-effective solutions to our climate problem."

An IEA Workshop on "Experience Curves for Policy Making – The Case of Energy Technology" was held in Stuttgart, Germany, May 10-11, 1999. The Workshop observed that "Experience curves provides the policy analyst with a tool to explore technology and policy options to support the transformation of energy systems and markets towards sustainable development". The Workshop also observed that experience curves "help to clarify the potential benefits of deployment programmes and market transformation programmes" and that they can help to "identify low-cost paths to $CO_2$ stabilisation by the middle of the next century". However, the Workshop also noted that in spite of their wide use in industry, experience curves remains under-exploited for public policy analysis. To realise its full potential for energy technology policy, the experience curve methodology requires further development. An urgent issue is the need for quality-controlled and publicly available empirical information on experience curves for new environment friendly technologies. Other development areas include the handling of uncertainty, time-series of cost rather than price data, use of analogies and technology spill-over between industries and countries. Putting experience curves into the policy analysts toolbox thus requires considerable efforts to establish a database and develop the methodology.

The Stuttgart Workshop made four Recommendations:

1. that experience curves are used to analyse the cost and benefits of programmes to promote environment-friendly technologies and that the resulting analysis be provided to governments for possible use in deployment policies;

2. that the experience effect is explicitly considered in exploring scenarios to reduce $CO_2$ emissions and calculating the cost of reaching emissions targets;

3. that the International Energy Agency takes the initiative to establish an international collaboration on experience curves for energy technology policy analysis;

4. that this international collaboration is charged with the tasks of disseminating and developing experience curve methodologies for our two first recommendations, but also of studying the effects of technology spill-over and the needs for concerted action among governments to support global learning.

The outcome of the Stuttgart Workshop was reported to IEA/CERT at their meeting in June 28-29, 1999. Based on the third recommendation the Secretariat proposed that it should aid the setting up of an International Collaboration, which should work on experience curves for energy technology policy. IEA/CERT supported the Secretariat's efforts to set up the international collaboration.

EXCETP is a follow-up to the IEA/CERT decision. The following part of this document describes the tasks for EXCETP and the services EXCETP provides for its participants. The organisation of EXCETP is discussed in section 4 and is based on active involvement from the Secretariat and research co-ordinating role of International Institute of Applied Systems Analysis (IIASA).

## Tasks

The work is carried out in three tasks, "Case studies – Global Learning and Local Deployment", "Analysis for Policymaking" and "Guideline and Database for Experience Curves". The two first tasks serves two distinct sets of clients. Guideline and database serves the Participants in EXCETP. Figure C.1 summarises the relations between the tasks and indicates the external clients for the tasks.

### Task 1: Case Studies - Global Learning and Local Deployment

The purpose of this task is to further develop the experience curve methodology for policy analysis and apply this methodology to analyse the experience effects of deploying technologies or technological systems with large potentials in many countries. Examples of technologies are photovoltaics, wind power, biomass, advanced coal power plants, fuel cells, heat pumps, air conditioners, compact fluorescent lamps, high-temperature superconductors. Buildings, lighting, industrial processes and transports are examples of technological systems on the demand side.

Cross-country and cross-industry case studies of specific technologies or technology systems are important to understand spillover technology and the relation between local deployment and global learning. The learning potential for technologies with no or very little market

Figure C.1. Summary of Tasks and External Clients

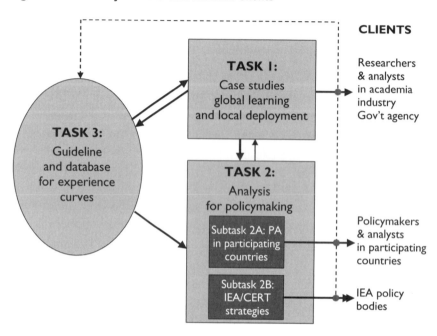

The dotted line indicate information feedback from the primary tasks 1 and 2 to the database task 3, which will function as a collective memory within the collaboration.

deployment can be estimated based on experience with similar technologies. The work will include both retrospective studies to establish an empirical base for analysis, and prospective or forecasting studies employing, e.g., scenario techniques to assess the effects of future learning. The empirical studies will give insights into the experience effect and provide parameters for the experience curves to be used in the prospective studies, but also provide information about the efficiency of policy measures to promote technology learning and make new technologies commercial. Prospective studies will make it possible to estimate the learning investments, investigate the efficiency of alternative policy measures and study the need for international collaboration to reach targets. Identification of niche markets is important in both types of studies.

Learning opportunities are scarce resources. Case studies will look at the competition for these resources among technologies and try to assess the cost-effectiveness of specific allocation of learning investments depending on the demands and objectives for the energy system. In a "Business-as-usual" case, markets are expected to provide an efficient allocation of learning opportunities. However, this allocation may not be cost-effective in the perspective of very long-range societal objectives, such as the management of the risk for climate change. Case studies on the competition for learning opportunities will provide indications for possible government intervention to promote environment friendly technologies, and help to identify possible technologies to be promoted. Results should also facilitate discussions about concerted action among governments on technology deployment policies.

Modelling techniques are important for studies of the experience effect. The case studies on the competition for learning opportunities require advanced energy systems engineering models. There are several research groups, which have developed or are developing different types of energy models with the capacity to study technology learning. It is important that the collaboration does not duplicate these efforts, but can access models already developed. Co-operation with external modelling groups will be mutually rewarding. From the database, EXCETP can provide an external partner with empirical data on progress ratios and entry points for energy technologies, and the case studies will provide benchmarks against which models can be checked.

Task 1 has a broad set of clients. It includes researchers in academia, industry and government agencies, who will act as peers to review the quality of the work. The ultimate goal of the work is to establish a database on energy technology learning and develop a methodology, which is useable for technology policymaking. Consequently, policy analysts are important clients of this study. They will act as peers to review the relevance of the work and will be the main users of the results. The results will provide insights into the mechanism of learning, but will not be specific enough to go directly into policymaking. Task 2 is therefore designed to provide direct links to the energy technology policymaking.

## Task 2: Analysis for Policymaking

The purpose of this task is to promote the implementation of experience curve methodology in a specific policy environment and use it as an analytical tool aiding specific decisions on energy technology policy. The clients are thus a specific set of policy makers and analysts. The work will draw on the achievements in Task 1, but requires active dialogues with the clients. Experience from this task will feed back to the studies in Task 1 and increase the relevance and improve the focus for these studies.

### Subtask 2A: Policy analysis in member countries

The purpose of this task is to disseminate, encourage and support the use of experience curve methodology for energy technology policy analysis and decision making in IEA Member Countries. The output should be a common framework and procedures within the participating countries for experience curve analysis to support policymaking. Pooling of dissemination and experience with the methodology reduce the country-specific cost of implementing the methodology. From an IEA perspective, the task facilitates discussions about concerted actions and common technology strategies.

The clients for this task are the energy policy makers and policy analysts in the participating countries. Part of the task is to design a process to reach out to the client and set the experience curve methodology on the agenda. National reference groups to follow the work within the collaboration have proven useful for dissemination and support in other IEA related work (e.g., ETSAP). The process could be initiated by seminars for the policy people within each of the participating countries building, e.g., on the work on experience curves within the Secretariat. To establish the methodology requires the country clients to commission studies and engage themselves actively in the outcome from such studies. Country studies would rely on results from task 1 and on the empirical data collected in the common database (Task 3)

### Subtask 2B: IEA/CERT strategies for co-operation on energy R&D and energy technology

The purpose of this task is to provide analysis to support IEA/CERT formulation of strategies for co-operation on energy RD&D and technology policy. The analysis will build on and integrate results from studies in Task 1 and national studies related to Task 2A. Interesting questions are, e.g., cost reductions through co-operation between countries, the need for concerted action among governments to accelerate learning or avoid lockout of environmental friendly technologies.

Clients are the IEA/CERT and its subsidiary bodies, but also other interested bodies at IEA may appear as clients. The work within this task will be carried out in close co-operation with the IEA Secretariat.

## Task 3: Guideline and Database for Experience Curves

The basic purpose of this task is to design, set up and maintain a quality-controlled database with information required to construct and analyse experience curves for energy technologies. The policy analysis in Task 2 and the case studies in Task 1 will draw on this database; however, individual work within these tasks will also generate new data that go into the database. This recycling of data is important because it opens all work to the same quality review procedures, makes data easily available to other members of the collaboration, and serves as a collective memory. Collecting new data is time consuming and expensive. Recycling will therefore be the most important modus of operation for the database in the first phase.

The control of data quality and use of the database require guidelines, which state what constitutes a proper and legitimate experience curve. Task 3 therefore includes the collection and synthesising of experience on how to measure and analyse an experience curve. This work will result in a short guidebook with a code of practice for constructing experience curves. The code of practice will serve as a standard for work within EXCETP. The need for such a standard emerges because the experience curve phenomenon still lacks a unifying theory, which, e.g., explains the form of the curve and can relate learning on different levels and between technologies as well as to other economic phenomena. The strength of the concept lies in the accumulated large body of empirical results, which can be used to benchmark learning for new technologies and as control for the quality of new studies. However, to achieve such benchmarking and control without a commonly accepted theory requires strict adherence to a well-documented and transparent methodology. Experience curves share this need for a code of practice to avoid confusing claims with, for instance, Life Cycle Analysis.

Task 3 provides service for Task 1 and 2. All the clients are therefore found within the collaboration. This, of course, does not reduce the requirement for both internal and external quality control and availability for peer review. Publication of working papers on experience curves available in the database facilitates external review. The guidebook with the code of practice for constructing experience curves also serves this purpose.

## Organisation

EXCETP is a *virtual organisation*, i.e., it has an identity of its own but all its members have their organisational home in other real organisations, which provide them with the resources to carry out their work. The concept of virtual organisations has emerged during the last decade within the management literature and been taken up in the business world as a way of putting the principle of flexible networks into practice in order to meet the needs of a rapidly changing environment. An early writer observed that "Virtual enterprises rely more on the knowledge and talents of their people that on the functions. Their managers, professionals and workers can multiplex their attention to multiple projects with different sets of project members during the course of a day, month, or a year."[34]

The identity of a virtual organisation is derived from common tasks, while much of the identity of real organisations is derived from common resources and functions. A virtual organisation is only viable as long as its members find that the tasks provides them with value added in the real organisation to which they belong. This means that the tasks must also provide value added to the real organisations and these organisations need to be aware or made aware of the value added. A virtual organisation, such as EXCETP, is thus free to define its tasks but depends for its survival that each home organisation for its members acknowledges the value of the tasks and is willing to support the execution of these tasks.

The organisation of a virtual organisation should be simple, and reflect the tasks and the reliance on home organisations for its members. Figure C.2 provides a simple layout of the organisation of EXCETP. Within the IEA structure, the Committee of Energy Research and Technology (IEA/CERT) is the client for EXCETP. IEA/CERT receives reports and evaluations via the IEA Secretariat, who also monitors activities and serves as overall co-ordinator of the work. However, each national or EU member of EXCETP should have contact directly or via the home organisation with the national or EU delegate to IEA/CERT. The full drawn lines in Figure C.2 thus represent conversations between EXCETP and its client, the dotted lines represent conversations between individual members of EXCETP and their clients, represented by the respective IEA/CERT delegate.

Within the IEA Secretariat, the project on Technology Learning[35] will be responsible for contacts with EXCETP. This project will also participate in the analytical work of EXCETP.

IIASA is the International Institute for Applied Systems Analysis in Laxenburg, Austria. IIASA is an international research institute, which

---

34. C. Savage, *Fifth generation Management*, Digital Press, Burlington, MA, 1990.
35. Project 16.8 in the document IEA/GB(99)50/ANNI

Figure C.1.  Major Communication Channels for EXCETP

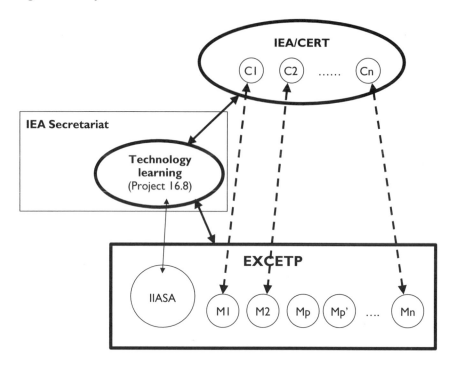

C1, C2.. are country and EU delegates to IEA/CERT. M1, M2.. are members of EXCETP coming from home organisations with government funding from respective countries or EU. EXCETP is open to persons from private industry, represented in the figure by Mp, Mp'.. "IIASA" refers to members in EXCETP from the International Institute for Applied Systems Analysis.

has been active within the field of technology learning since it was started in 1972. Within EXCETP, members from IIASA will participate in the analytical work but also contribute to the scientific co-ordination of the collaboration.

## *Funding*

There is no common funding for EXCETP; each member receives all his resources from his home organisation. The home organisations are responsible for securing necessary funding, either within their own budgets or from external sources. IIASA as an international research organisation has the option of applying for funds by national research foundations in the participating countries and by private sources.

The IEA Secretariat cannot support EXCETP from its regular budget, but requires voluntary contributions from the participating countries to manage the network, report to IEA/CERT and do its share in the tasks.

# Order Form

**OECD BONN CENTRE**

c/o DVG mbh (OECD)
Birkenmaarstrasse 8
D-53340 Meckenheim, Germany
Tel: (+49-2225) 926 166
Fax: (+49-2225) 926 169
E-mail: oecd@dvg.dsb.net
Internet: www.oecd.org/bonn

**OECD MEXICO CENTRE**

Edificio INFOTEC
Av. San Fernando No. 37
Col. Toriello Guerra
Tlalpan C.P. 14050, Mexico D.F.
Tel: (+52-5) 528 10 38
Fax: (-52-5) 606 13 07
E-mail: mexico.contact@oecd.org
Internet: rtn.net.mx/ocde

## OECD CENTRES

*Please send your order
by mail, fax, or by e-mail
to your nearest
OECD Centre*

**OECD TOKYO CENTRE**

Landic Akasaka Building
2-3-4 Akasaka, Minato-ku
Tokyo 107-0052, Japan
Tel: (+81-3) 3586 2016
Fax: (+81-3) 3584 7929
E-mail: center@oecdtokyo.org
Internet: www.oecdtokyo.org

**OECD WASHINGTON CENTER**

2001 L Street NW, Suite 650
Washington, D.C., 20036-4922, US
Tel: (+1-202) 785-6323
Toll-free number for orders:
(+1-800) 456-6323
Fax: (+1-202) 785-0350
E-mail: washington.contact@oecd.org
Internet: www.oecdwash.org

*I would like to order the following publications*

| PUBLICATIONS | ISBN | QTY | PRICE | | TOTAL |
|---|---|---|---|---|---|
| ☐ Experience Curves for Energy Technology Policy | 92-64-17650-0 | | $80.00 | FF 580 | |
| ☐ World Energy Outlook: 1999 Insights | 92-64-17140-1 | | $120.00 | FF 750 | |
| ☐ Electric Power Technology: Opportunities and Challenges of Competition | 92-64-17133-9 | | $40.00 | FF 250 | |
| ☐ International Collaboration in Energy Technology | 92-64-17057-X | | $120.00 | FF 680 | |
| ☐ Coal Information 1998 | 92-64-17087-1 | | $200.00 | FF 1200 | |
| ☐ Electricity Information 1998 | 92-64-17089-8 | | $130.00 | FF 800 | |
| ☐ Natural Gas Information 1998 | 92-64-17088-X | | $150.00 | FF 930 | |
| ☐ Oil Information 1998 | 92-64-05863-X | | $150.00 | FF 930 | |
| | | | | TOTAL | |

## DELIVERY DETAILS

Name                                    Organisation

Address


Country                                 Postcode

Telephone                               Fax

## PAYMENT DETAILS

☐ I enclose a cheque payable to IEA Publications for the sum of $ _____ or FF _____

☐ Please debit my credit card (tick choice).    ☐ Access/Mastercard  ☐ Diners  ☐ VISA  ☐ AMEX

Card no: └─┴─┴─┴─┴─┴─┴─┴─┴─┴─┴─┴─┴─┴─┴─┘

Expiry date: └─┴─┴─┴─┴─┴─┘                Signature:

IEA PUBLICATIONS, 9, rue de la Fédération, 75739 PARIS CEDEX 15
PRINTED IN FRANCE BY STEDI
(61 00 02 1P) ISBN 92-64-17650-0 - 2000